View From The Sidewalk
A New York City Odyssey

There came a moment when it was clear that time does not always travel at a constant speed.

New York City was serene as spring debated whether or not it would appear.

Unencumbered by the usual mass of humanity, the City lay in peaceful repose, eagerly welcoming the exploration of its treasures.

The inspiration for this book is the result of many pleasant sojourns into that landscape, made more accessible by an unexpected and unprecedented amalgam of events.

From this point on, the pictures do a better job of explaining themselves than the words.

©2021 Daniel Pelavin
daniel@pelavin.com
all rights reserved

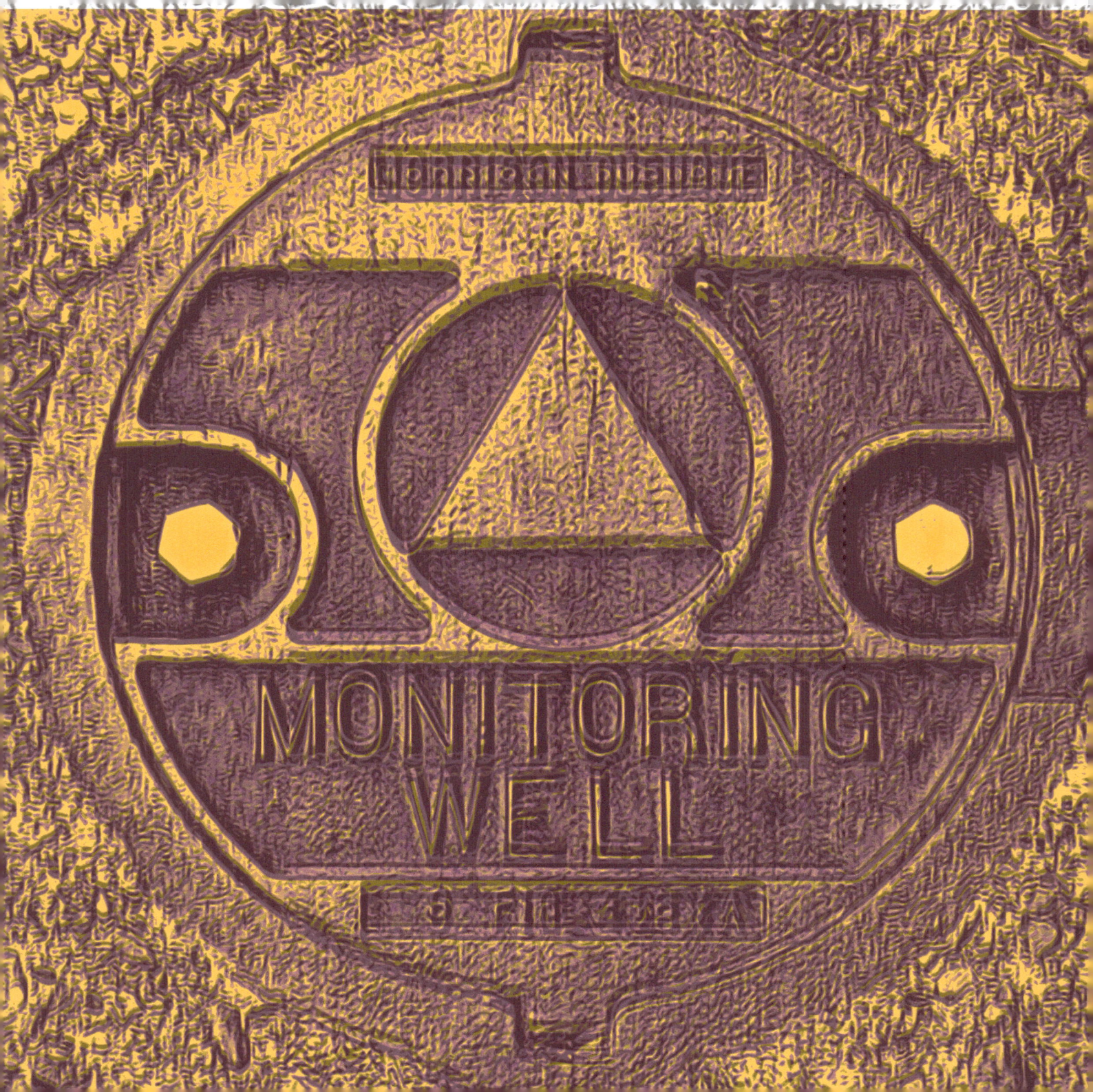

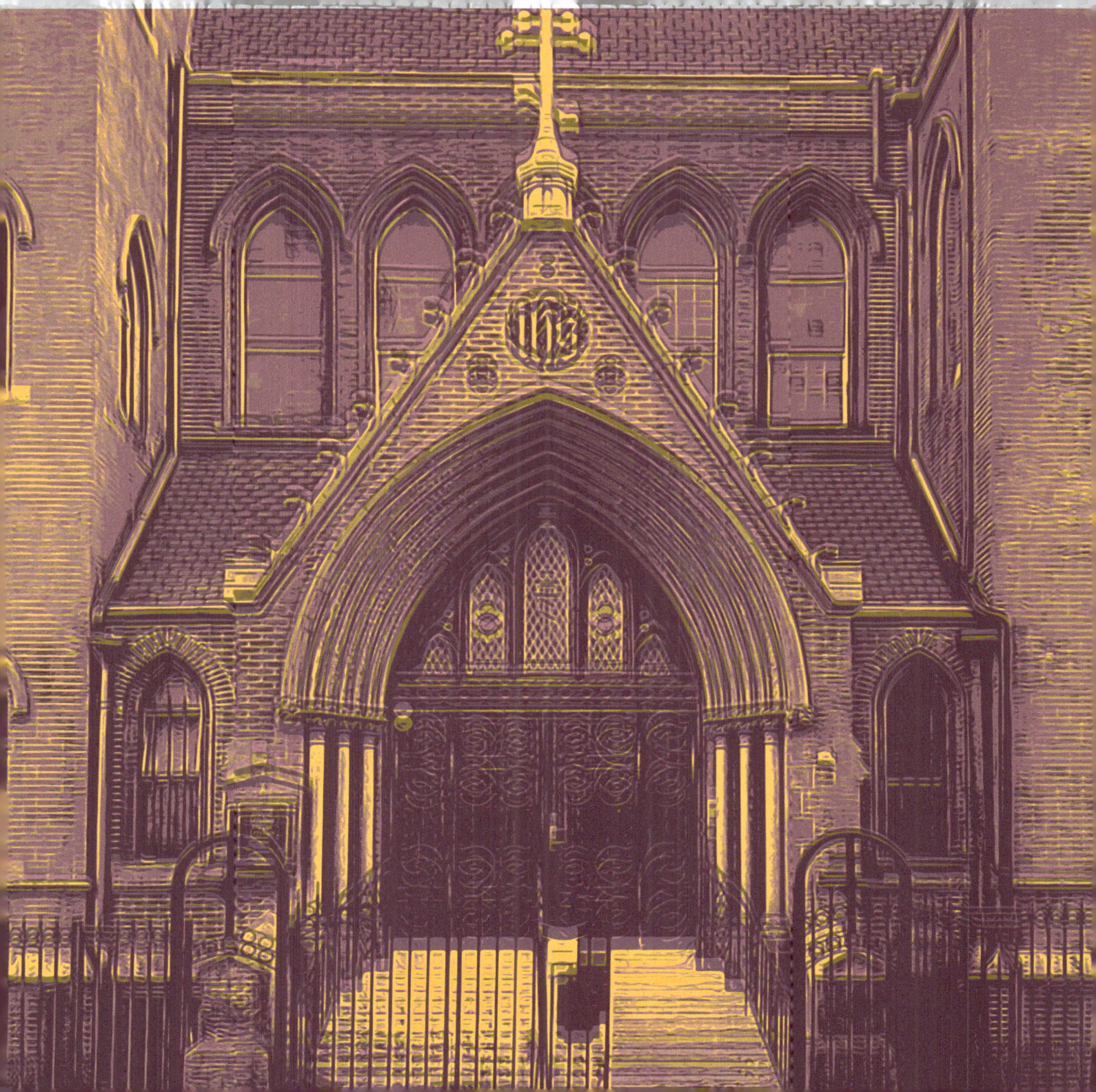

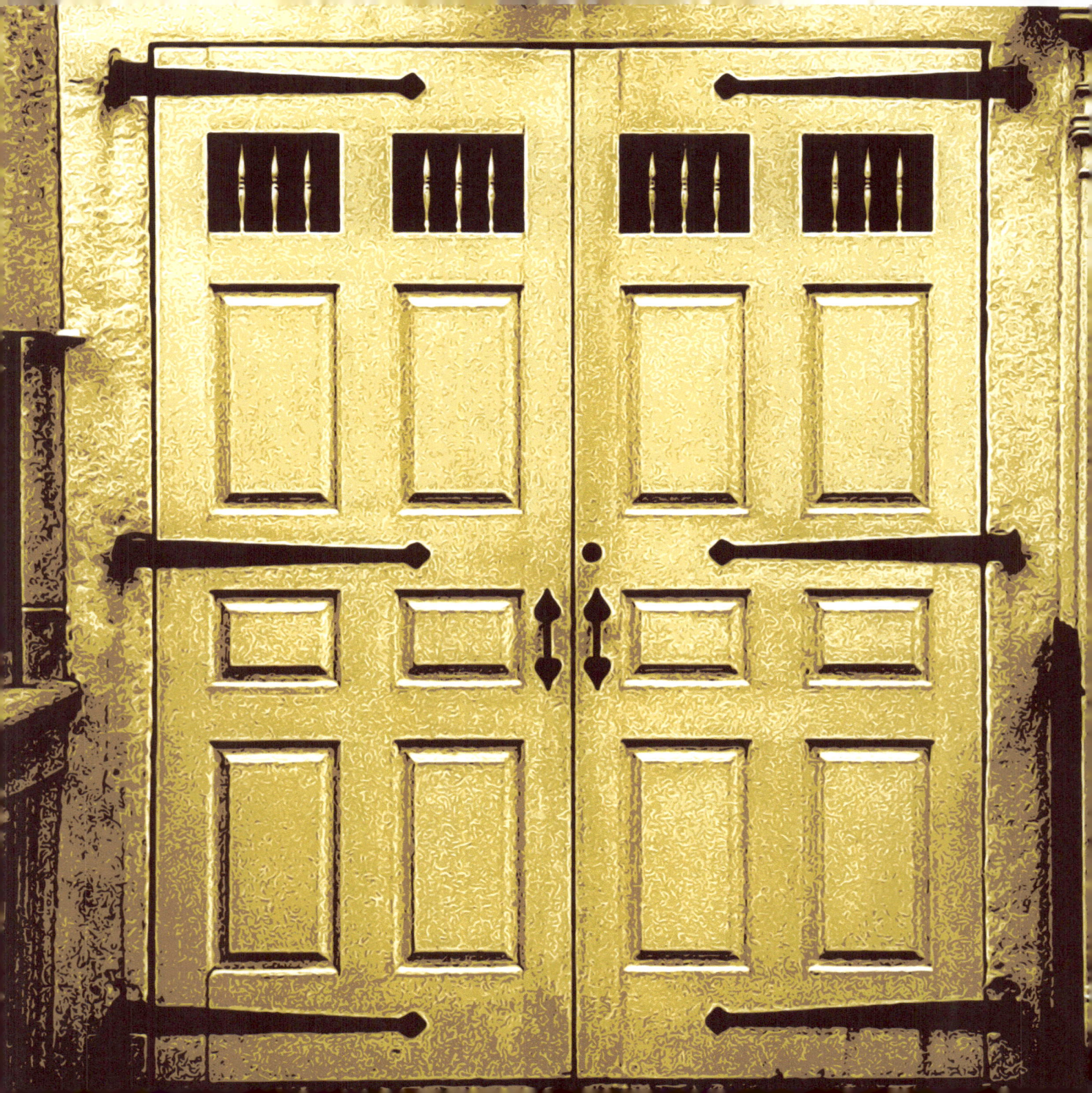

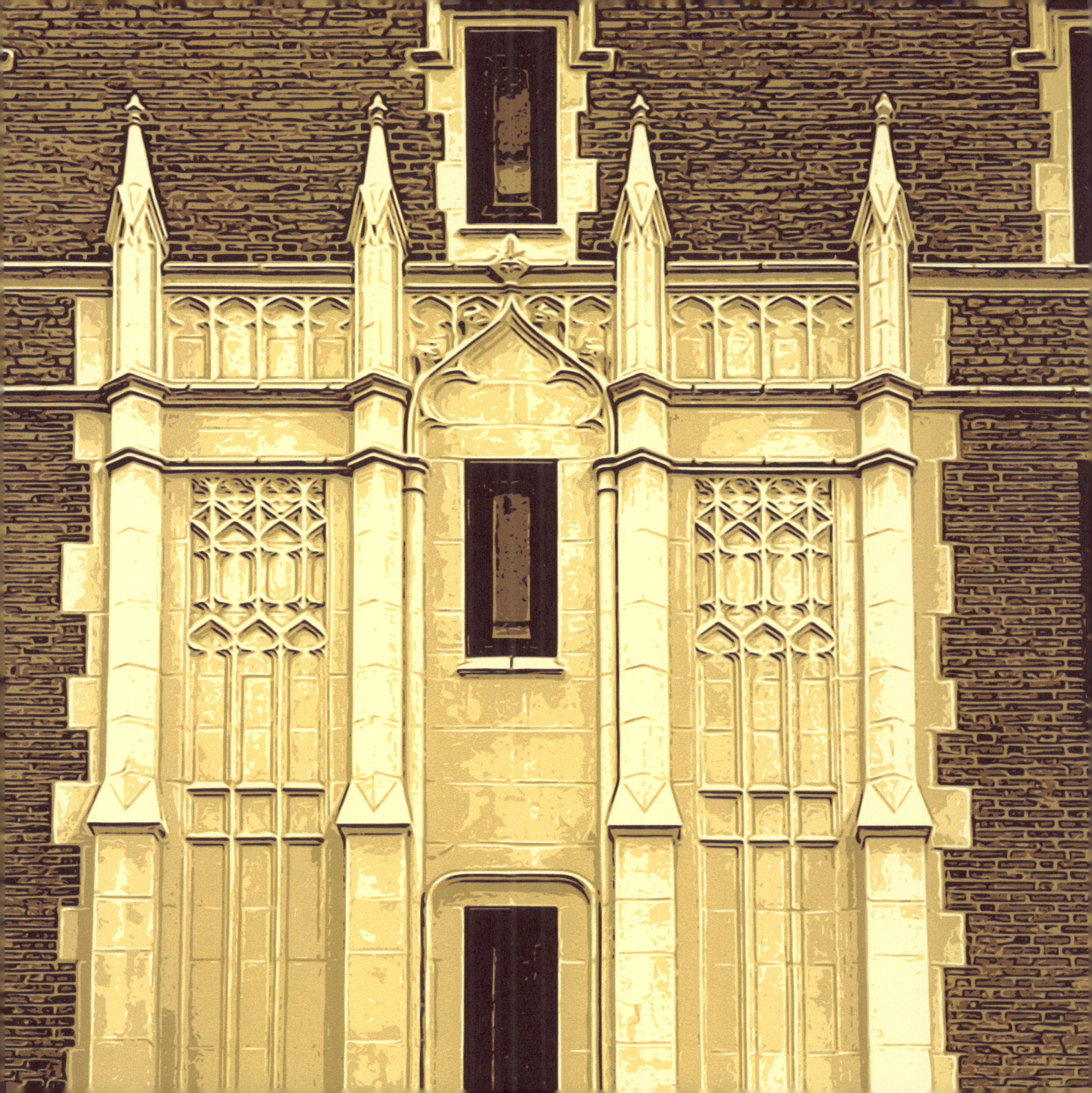

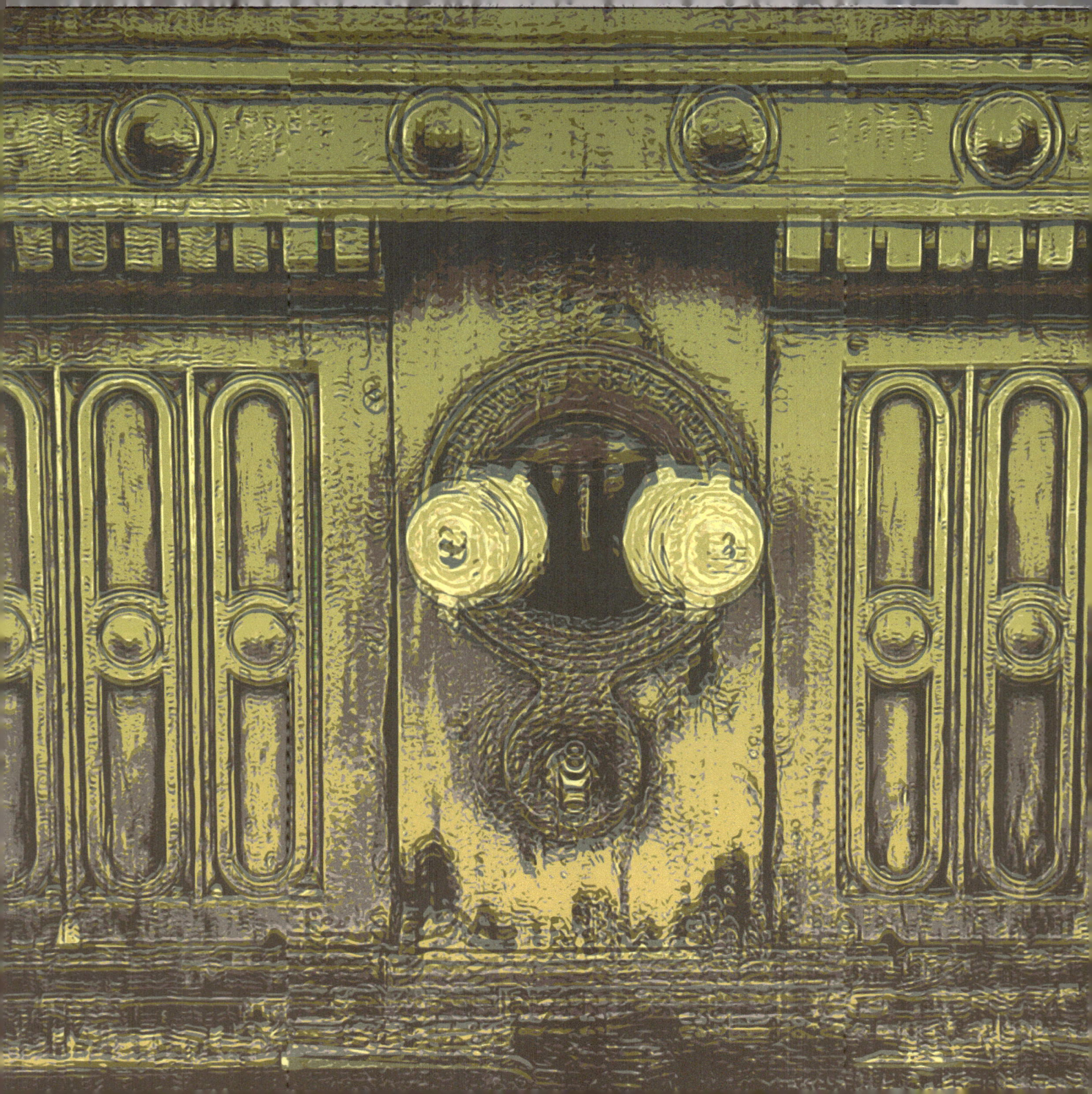

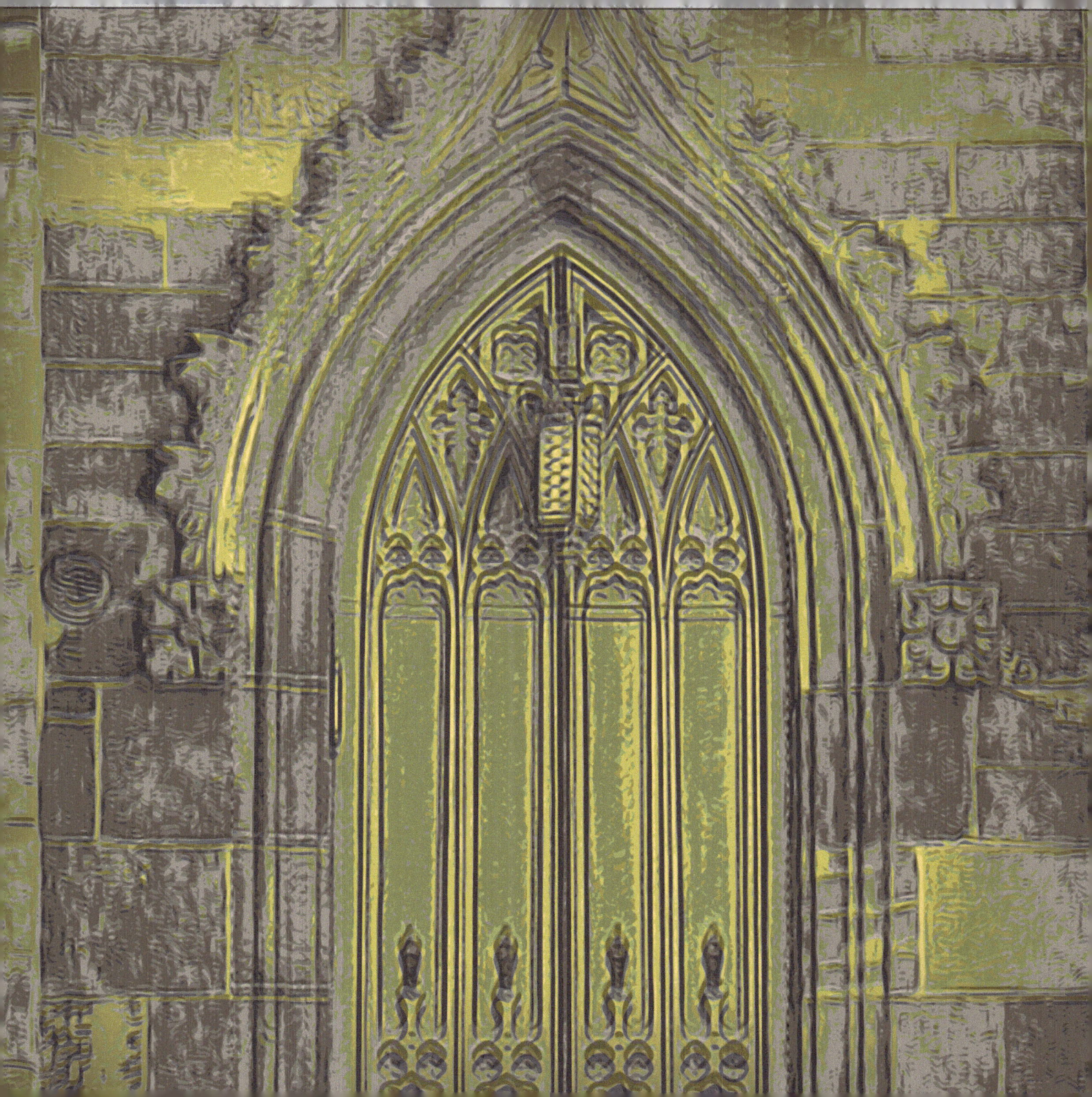

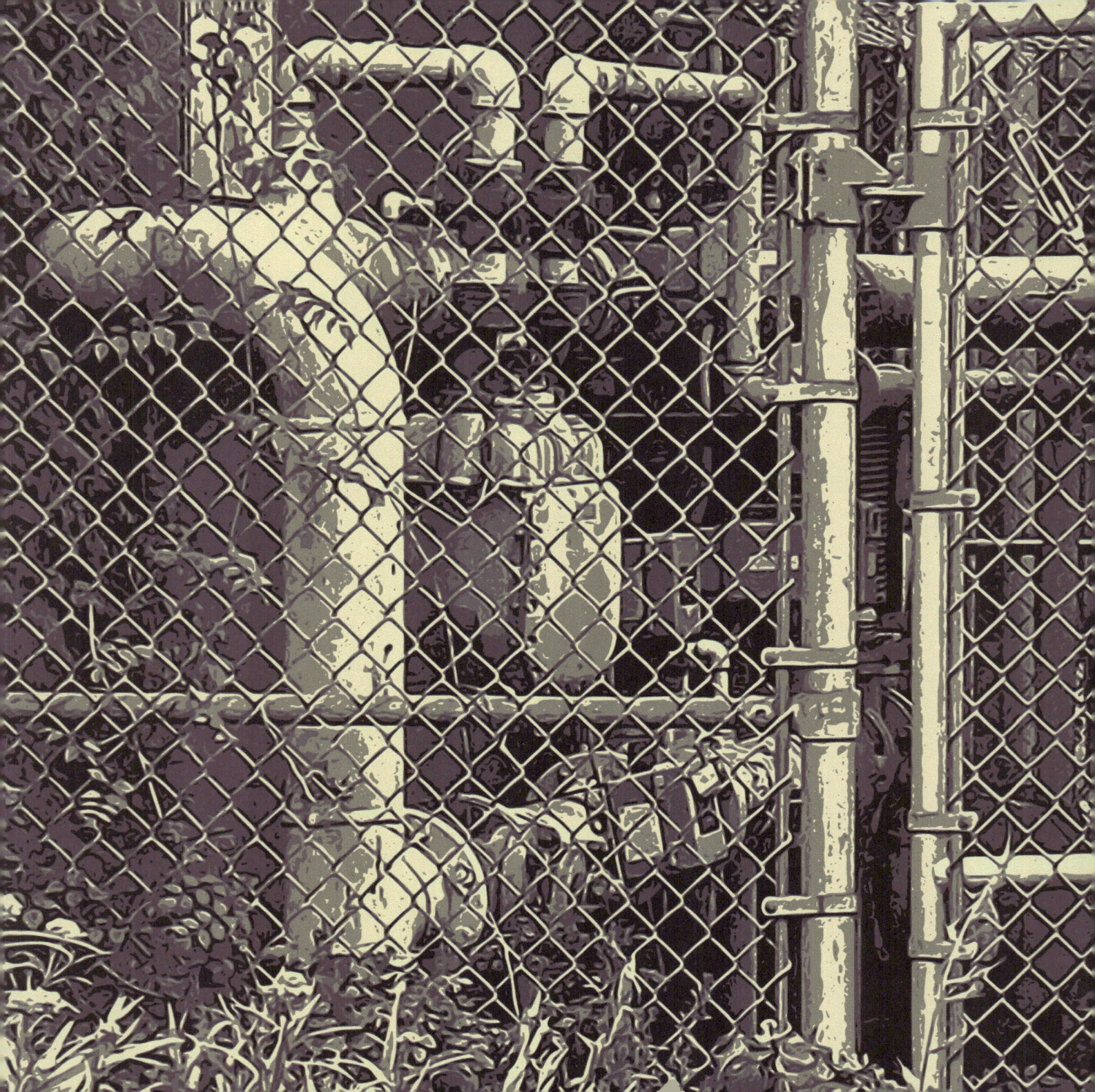

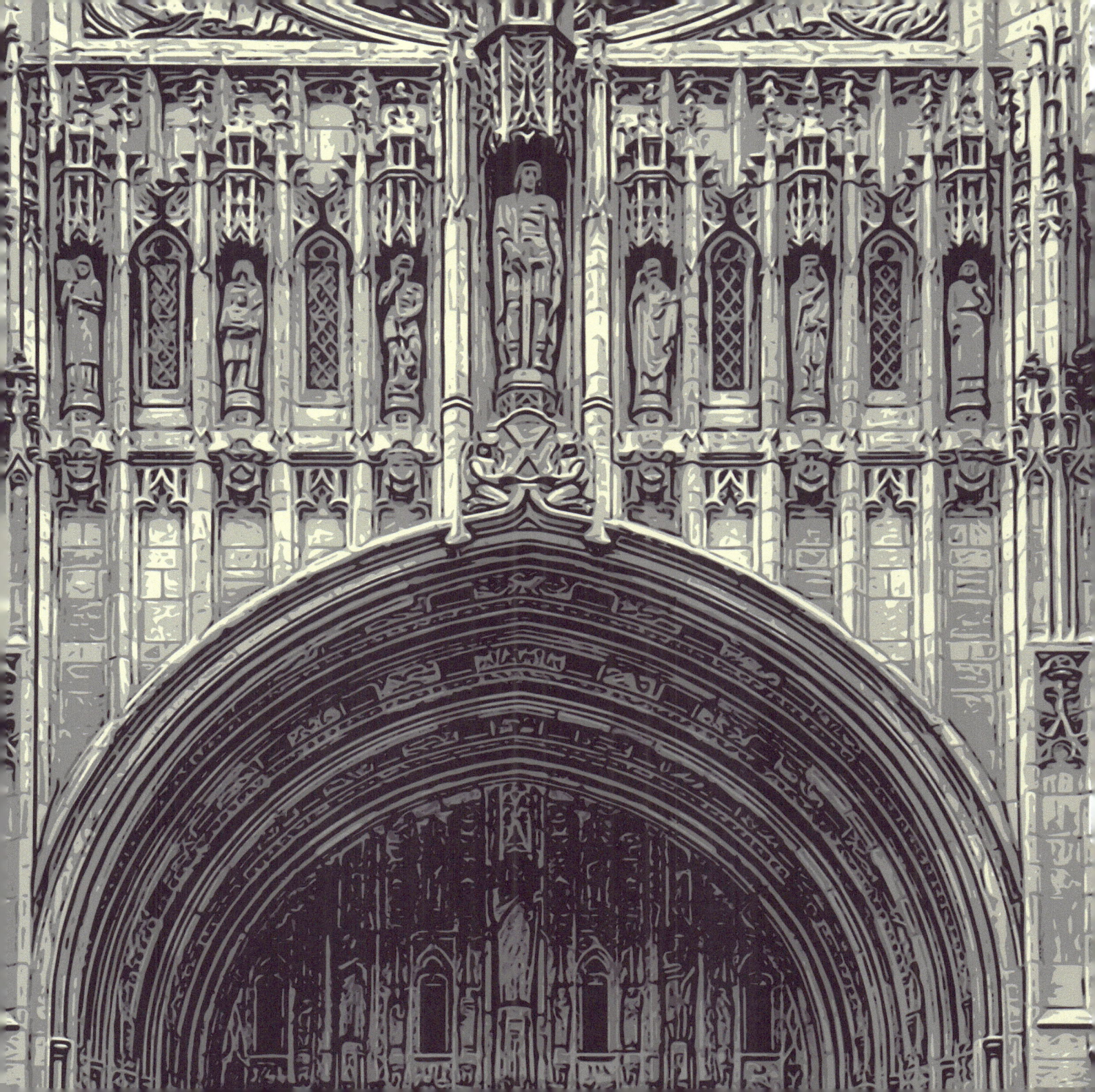

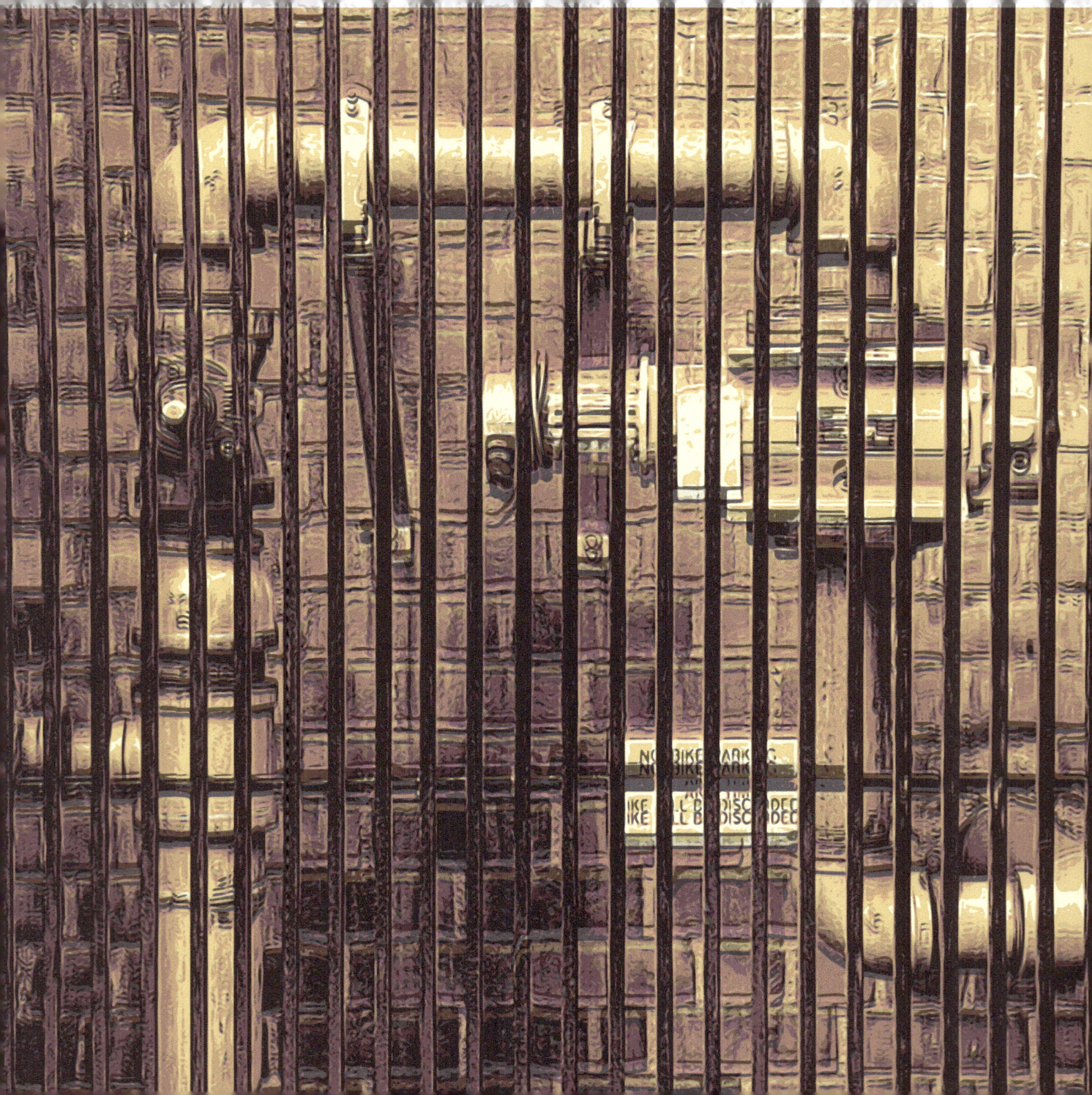

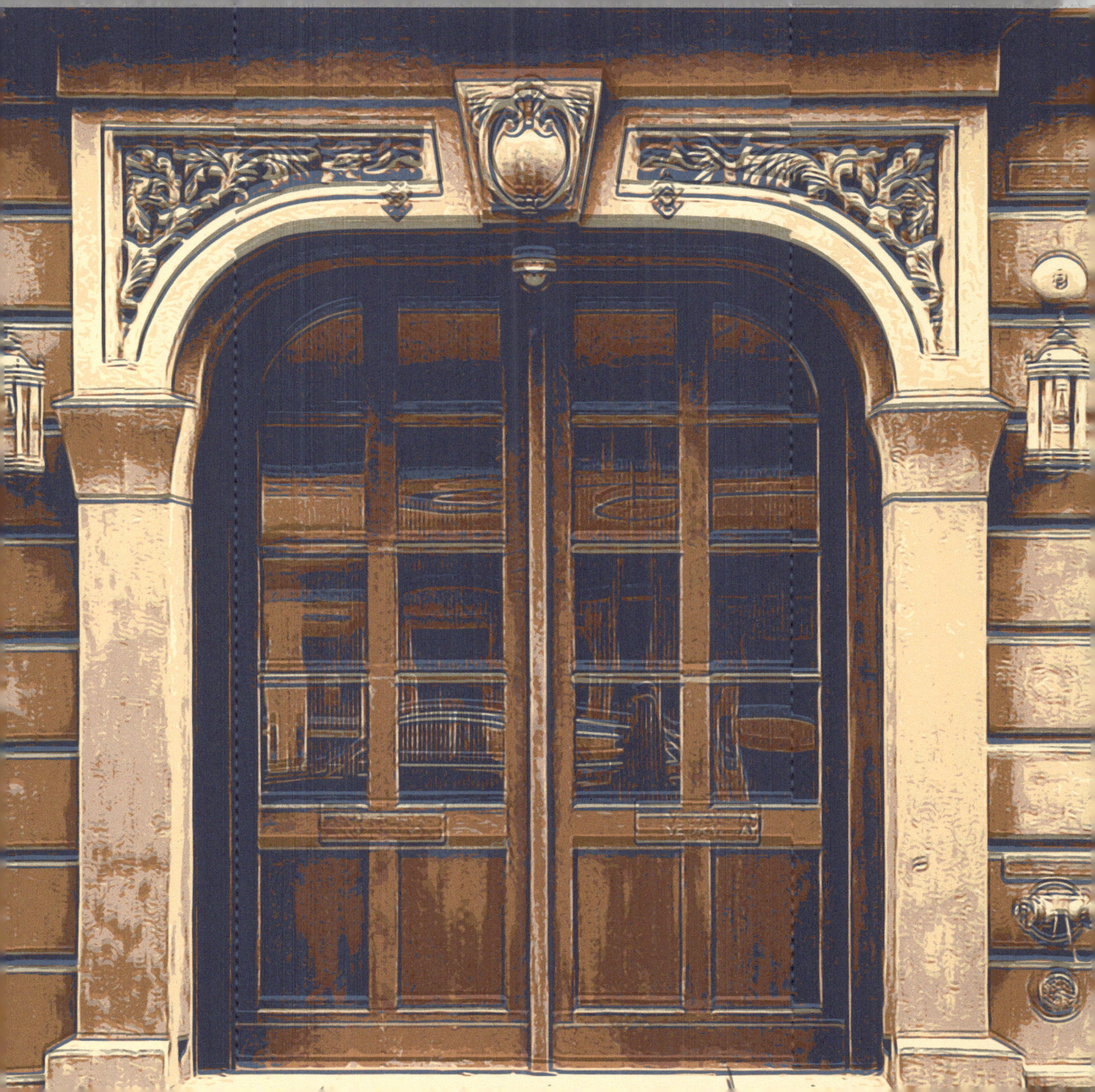

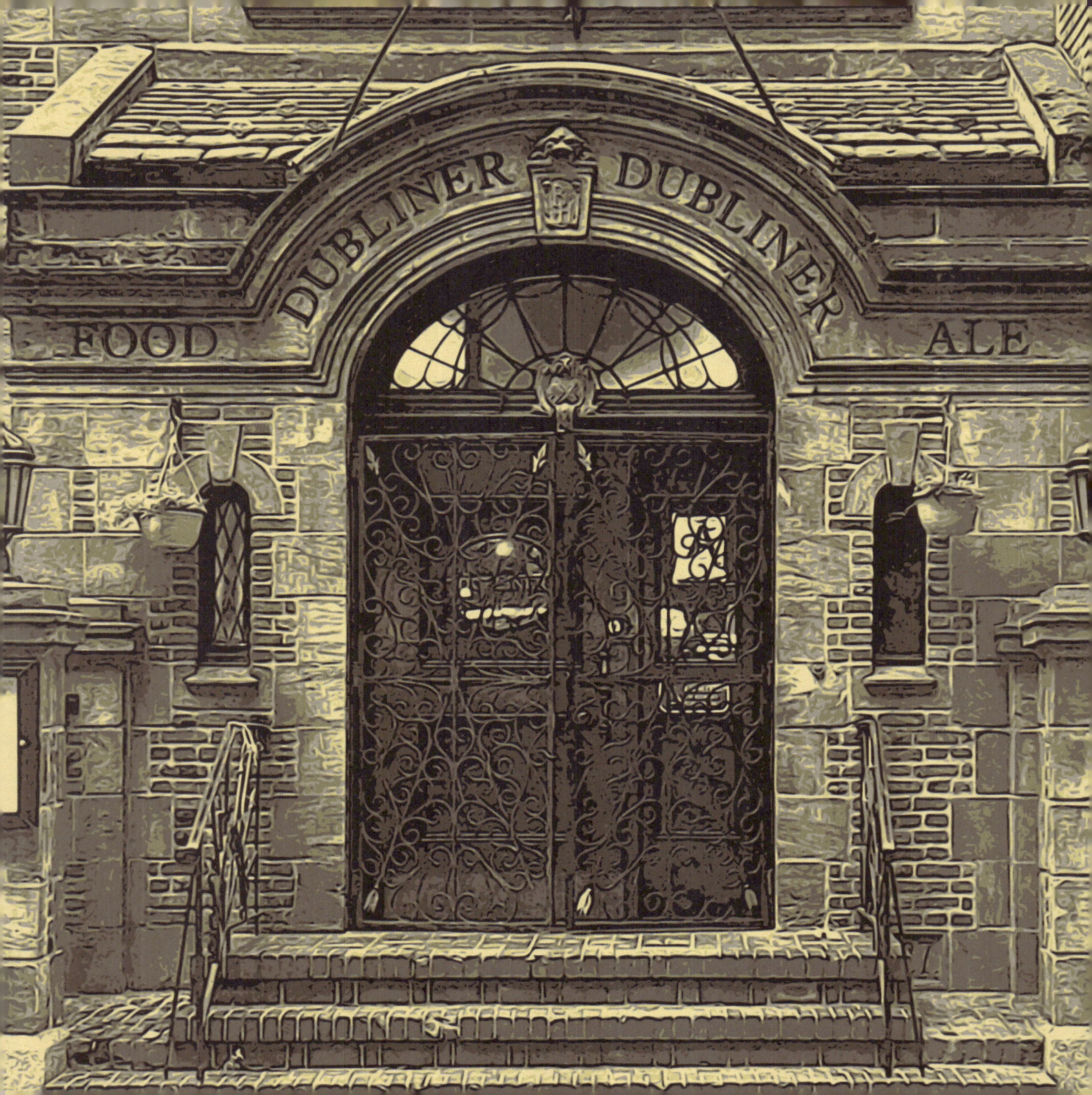

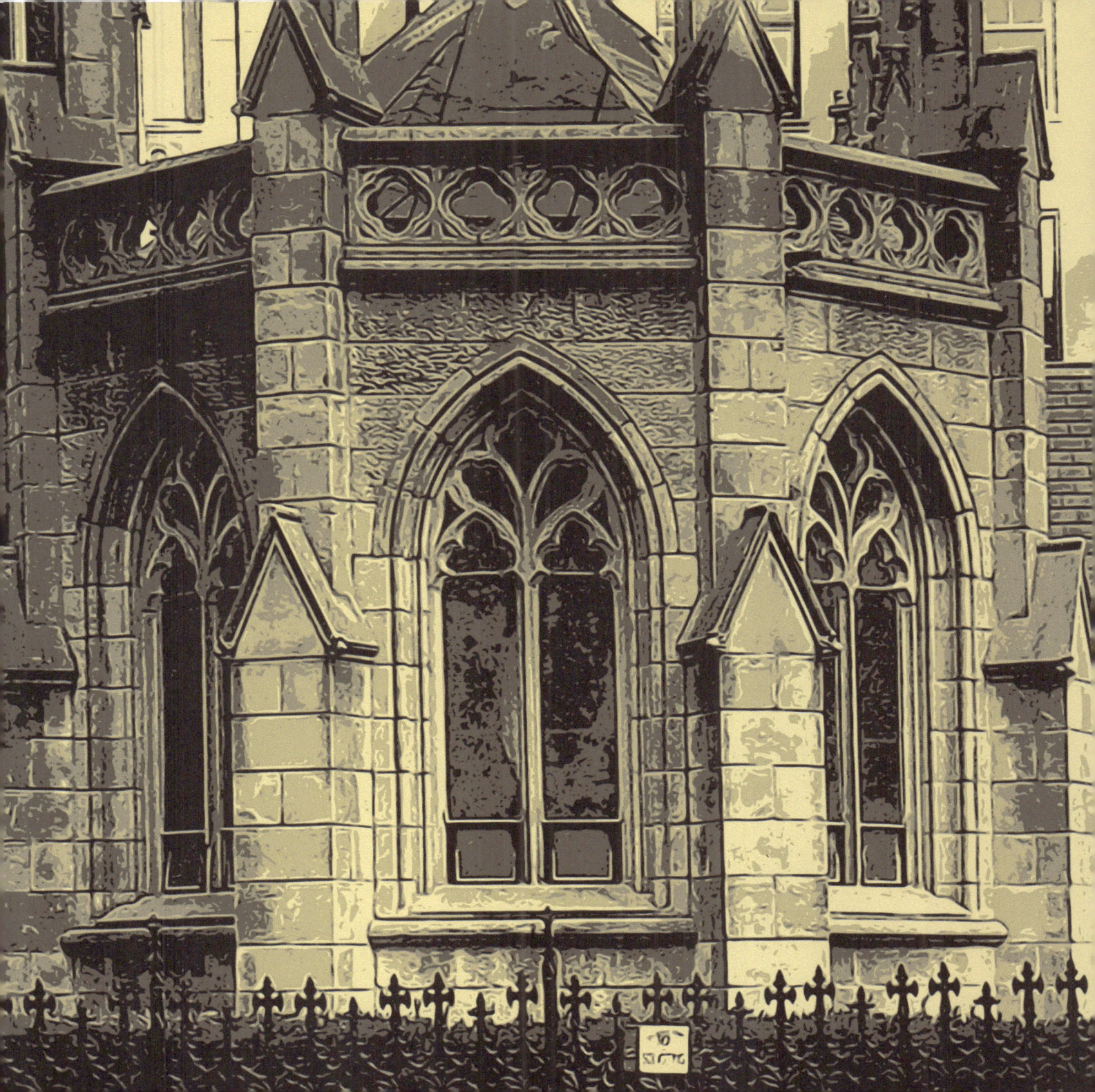

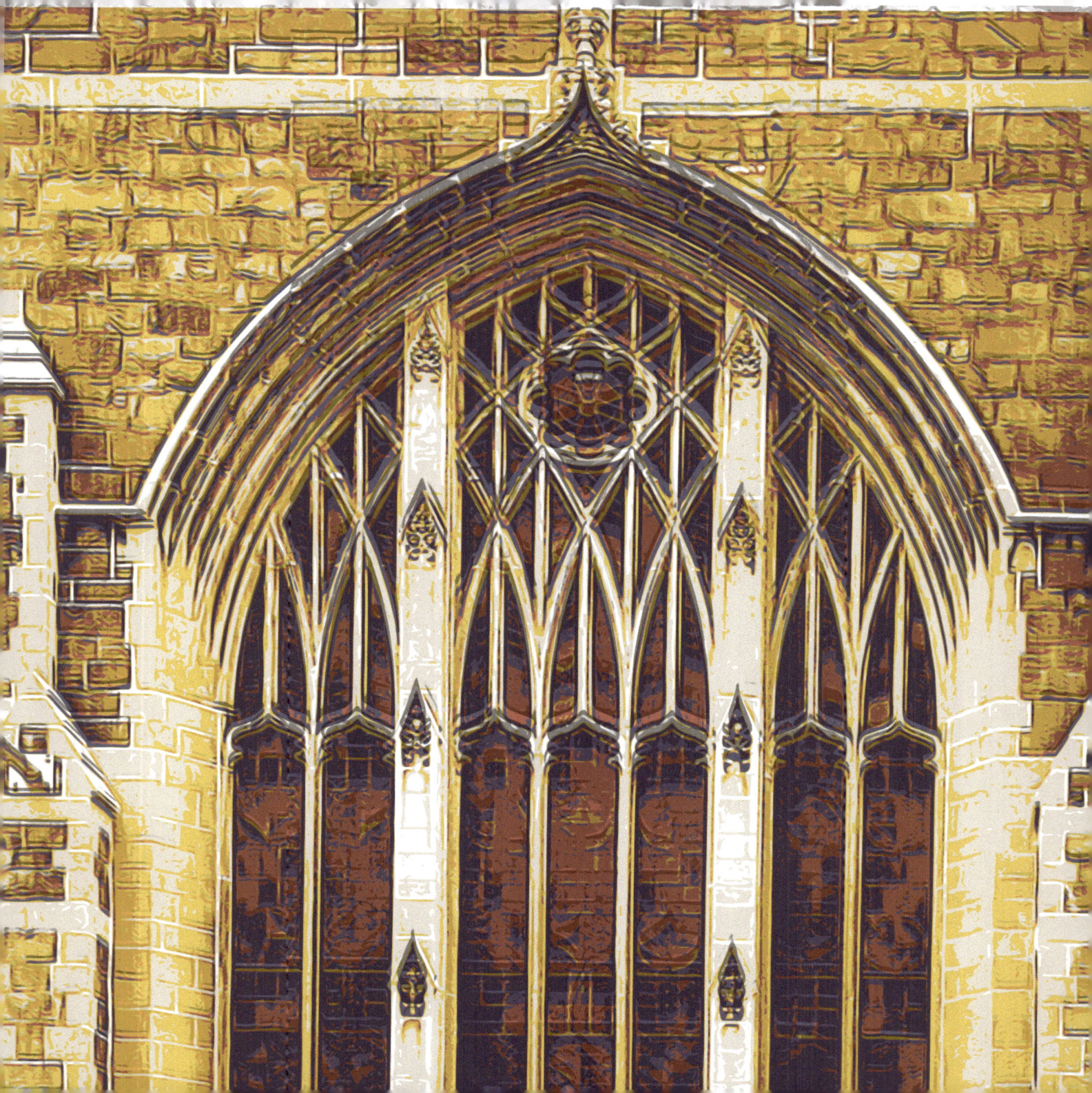

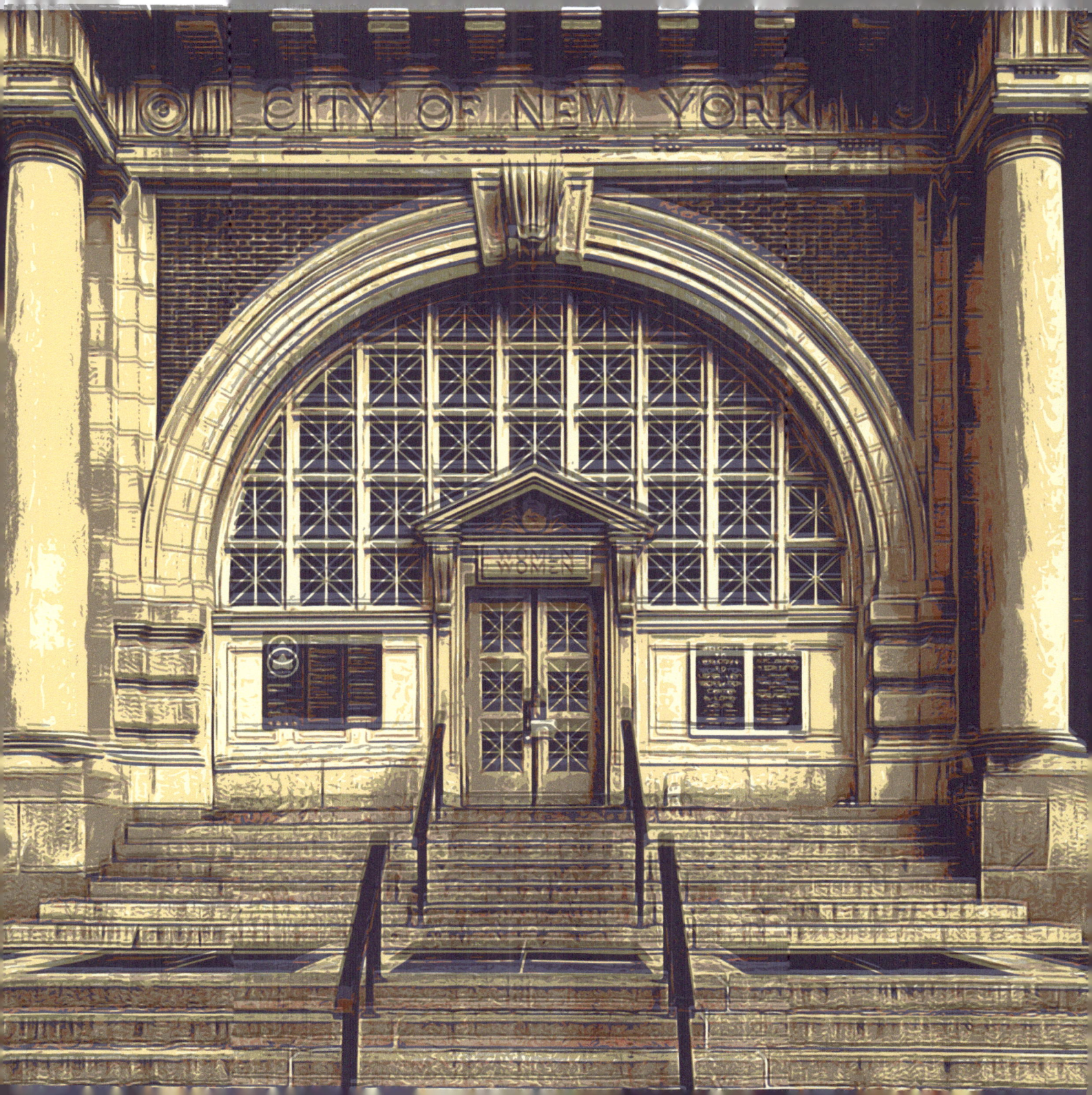

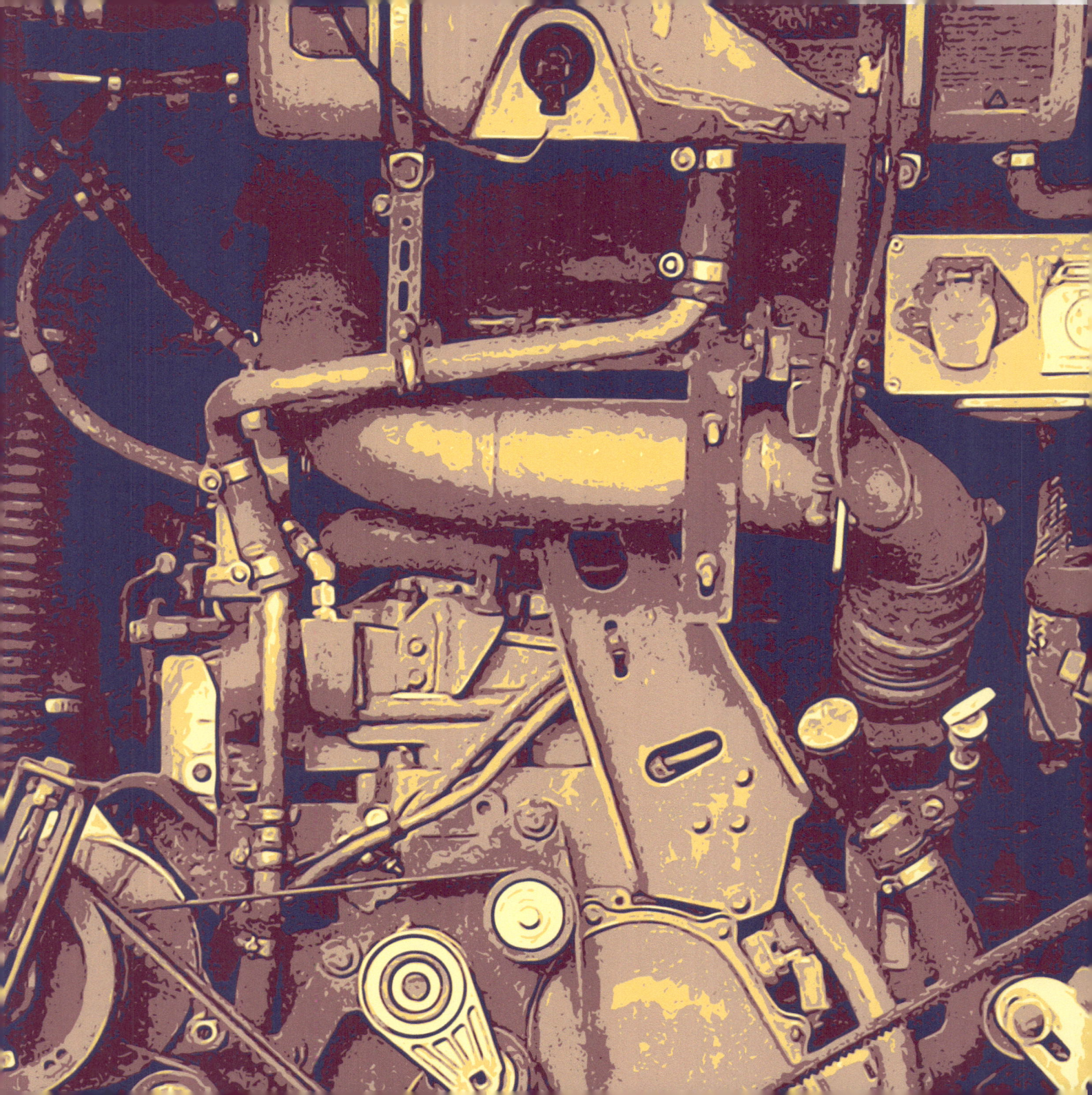

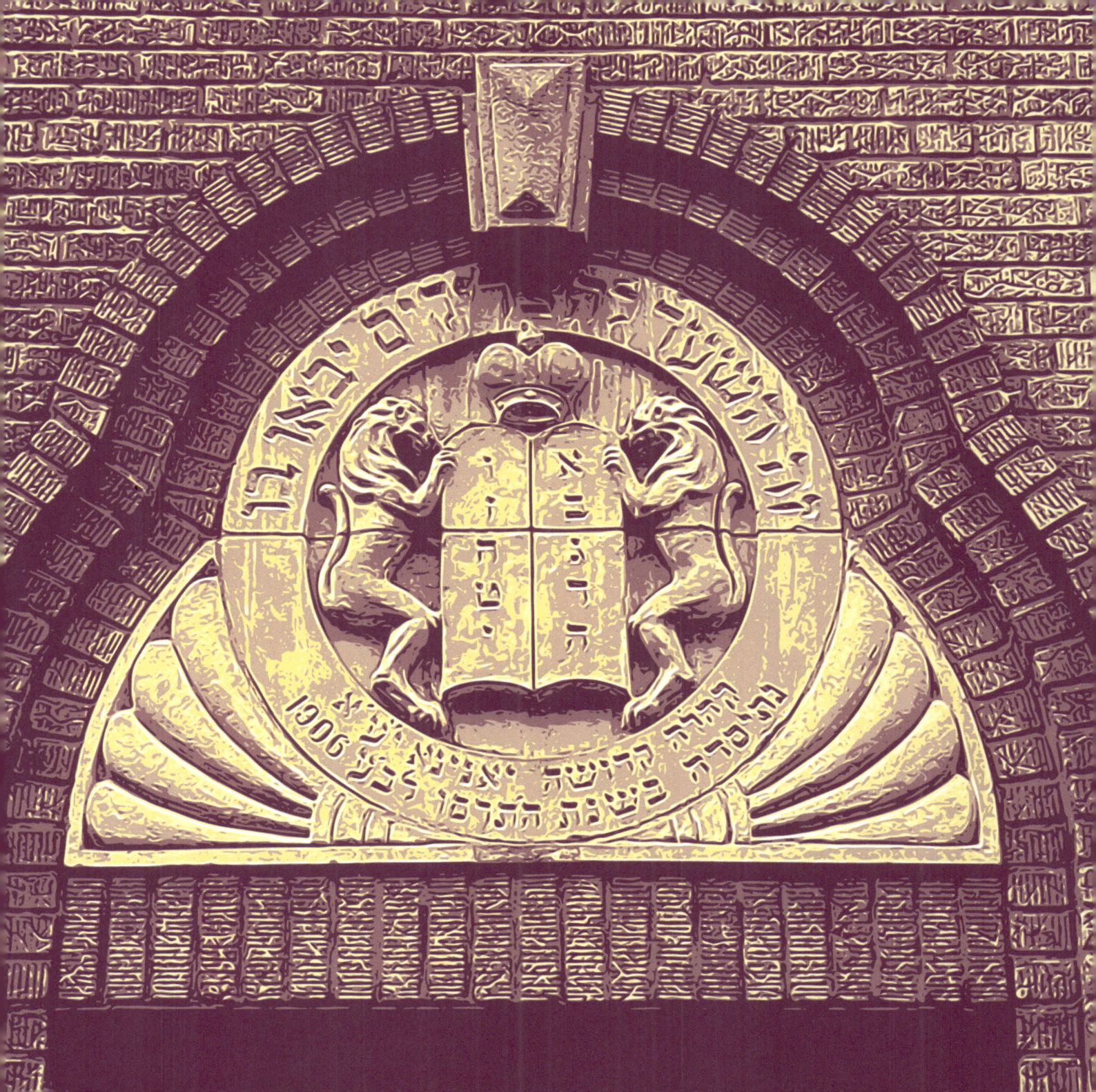

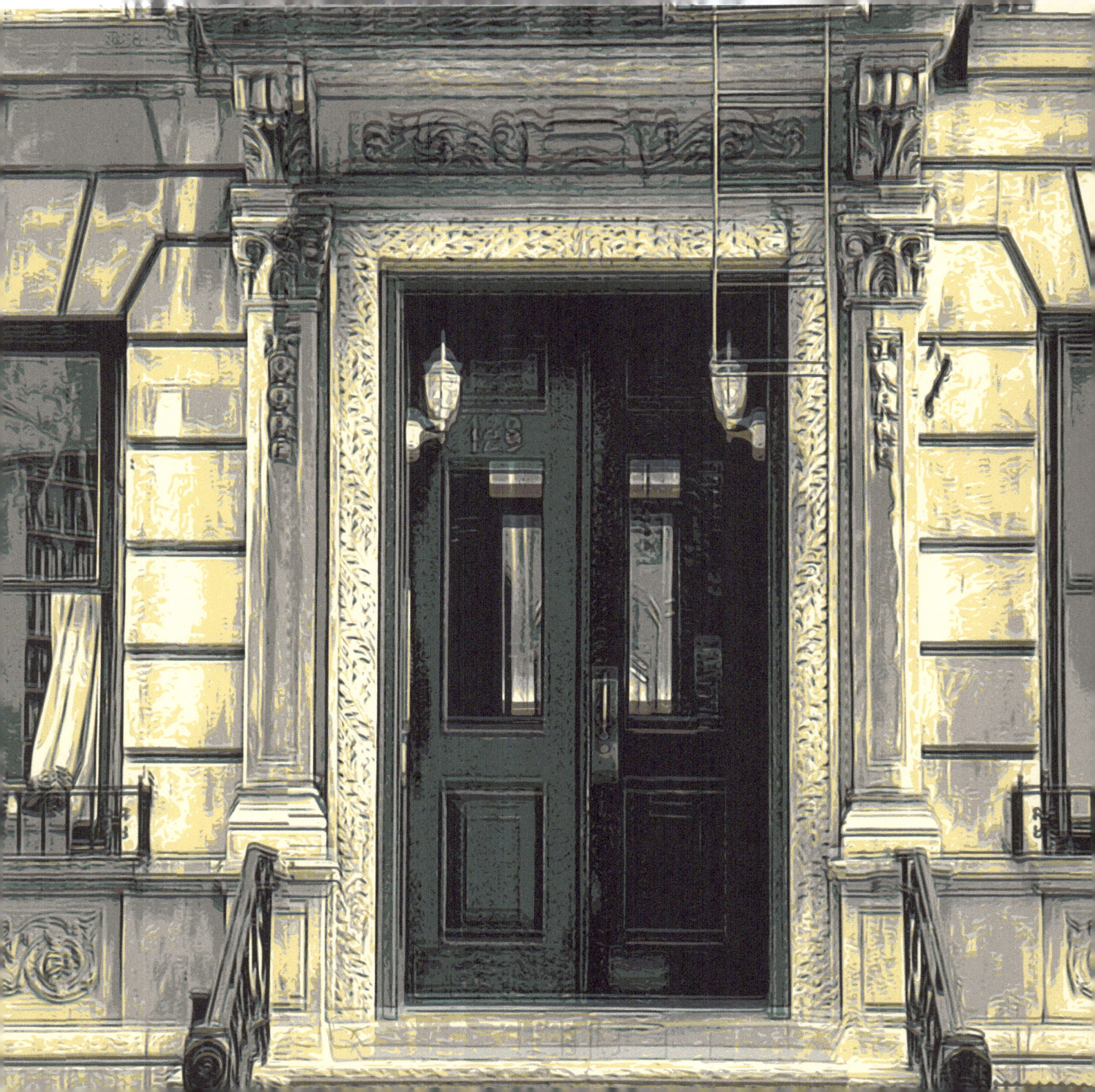

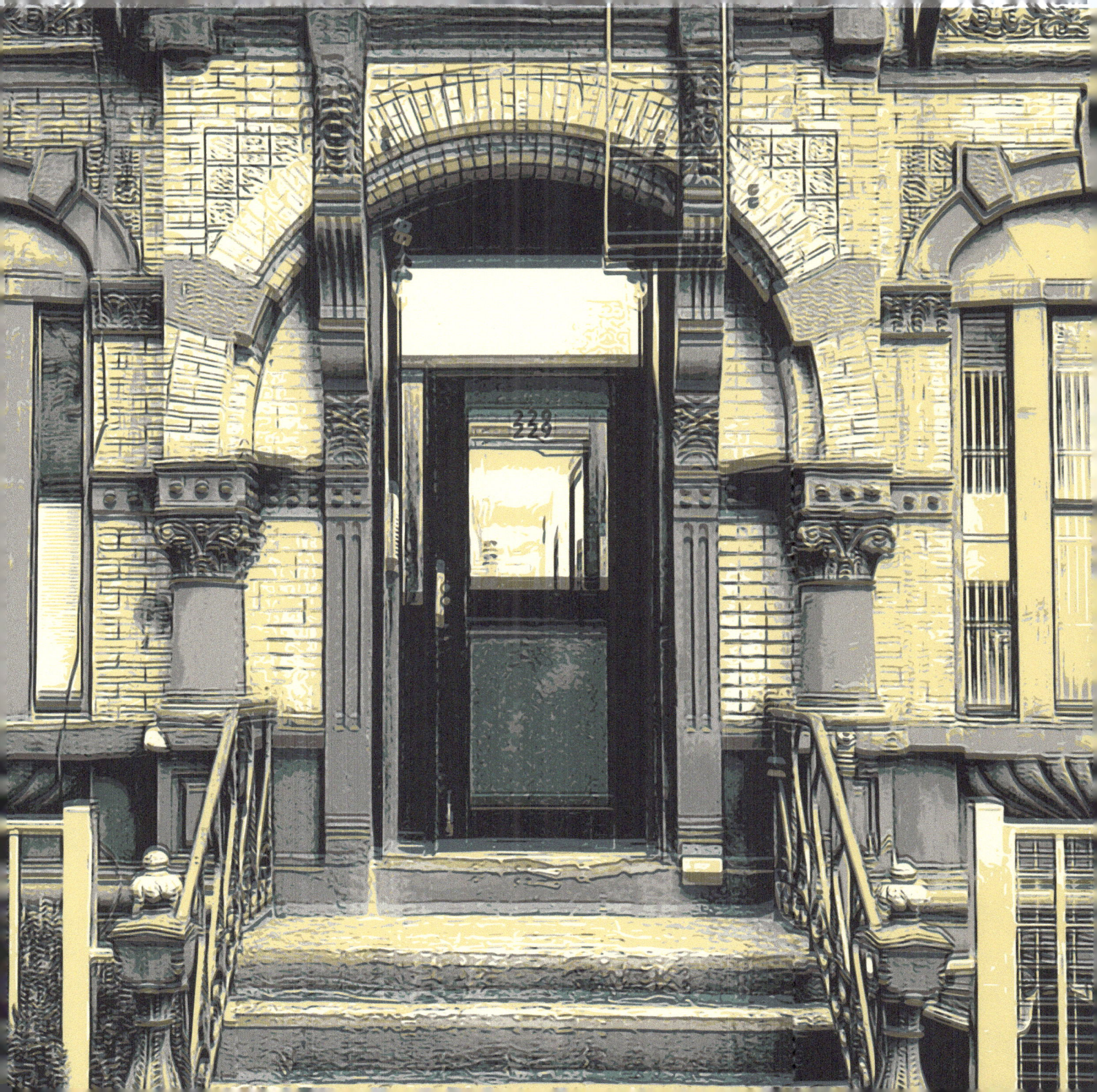

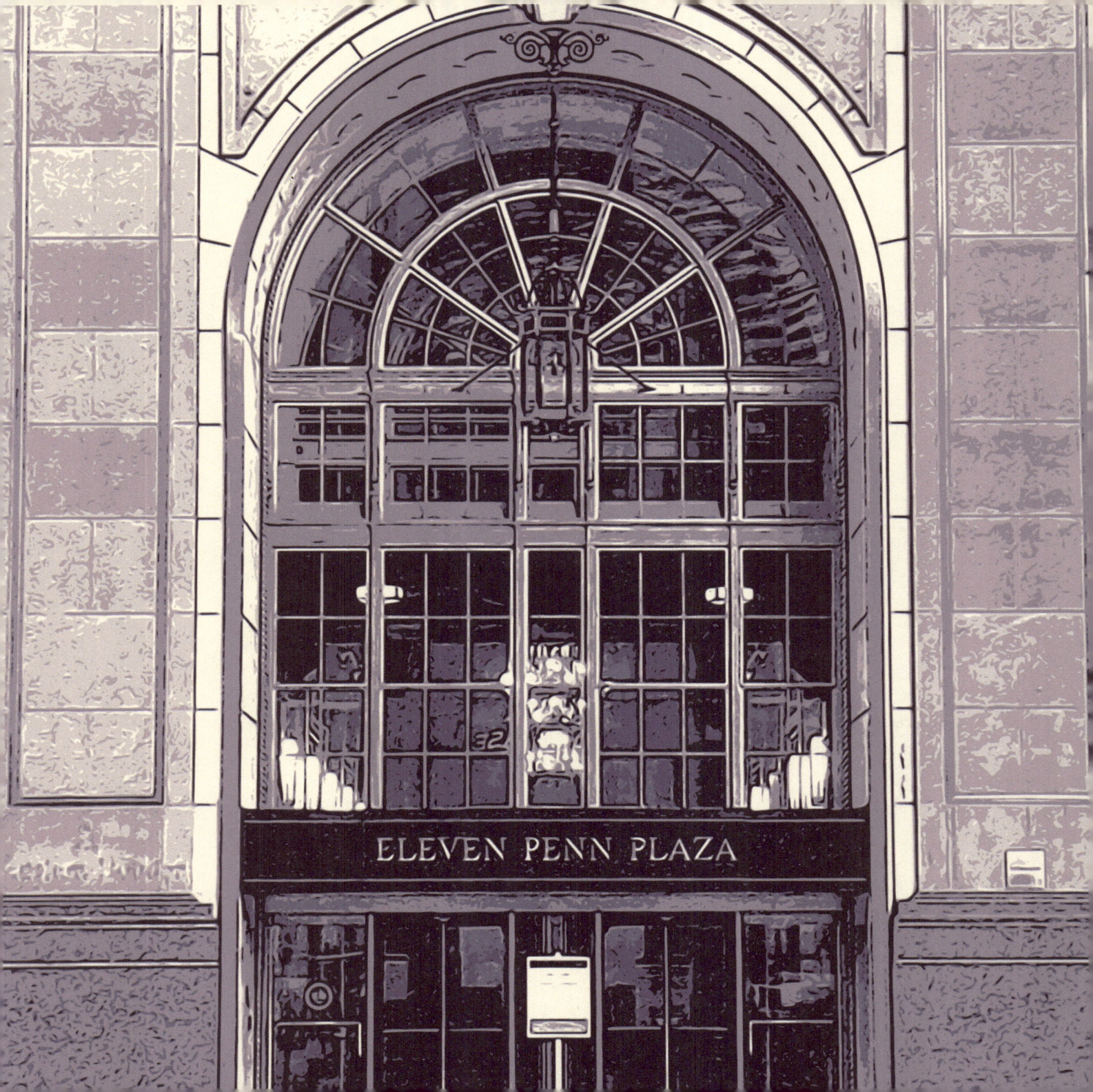

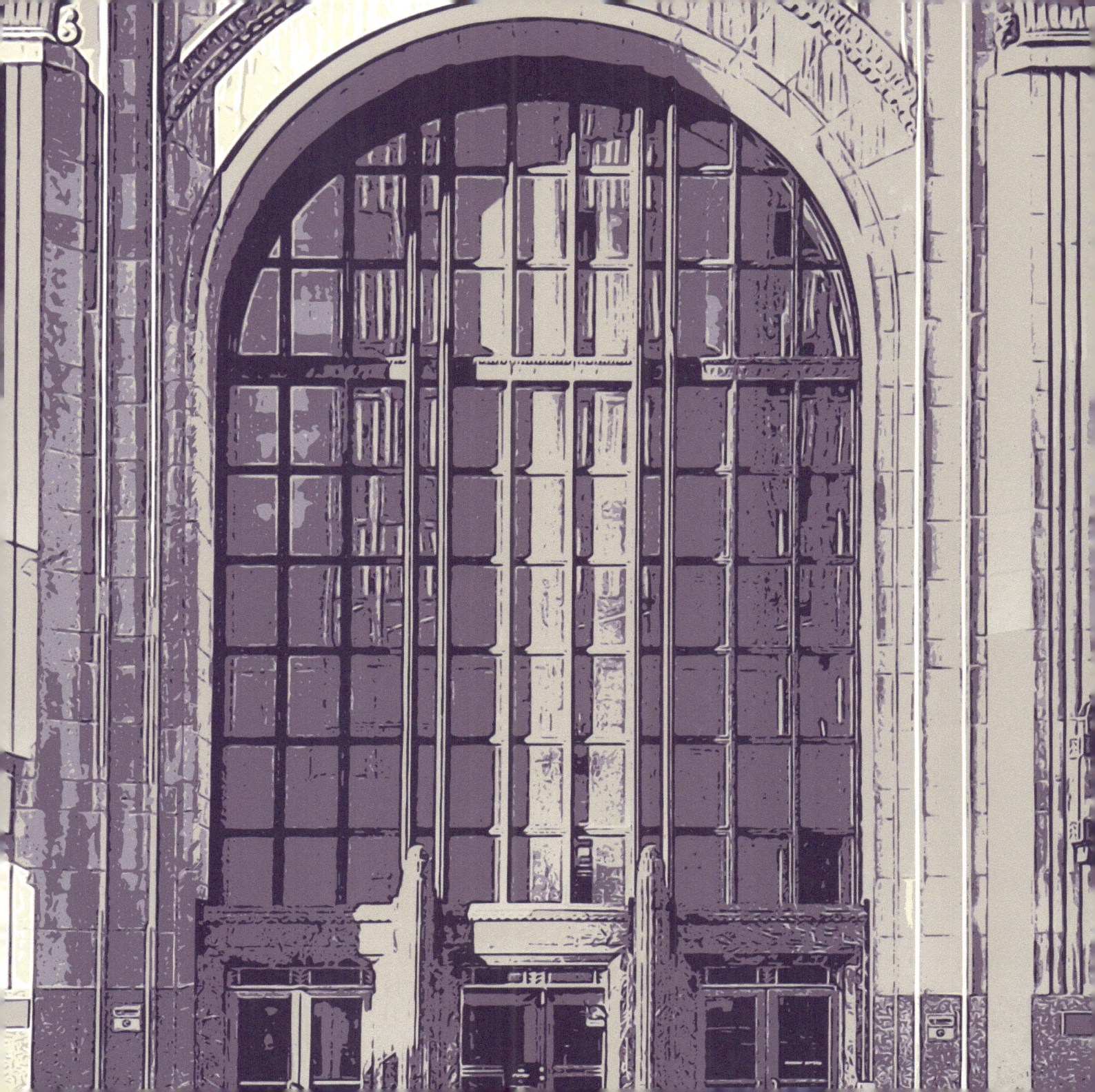

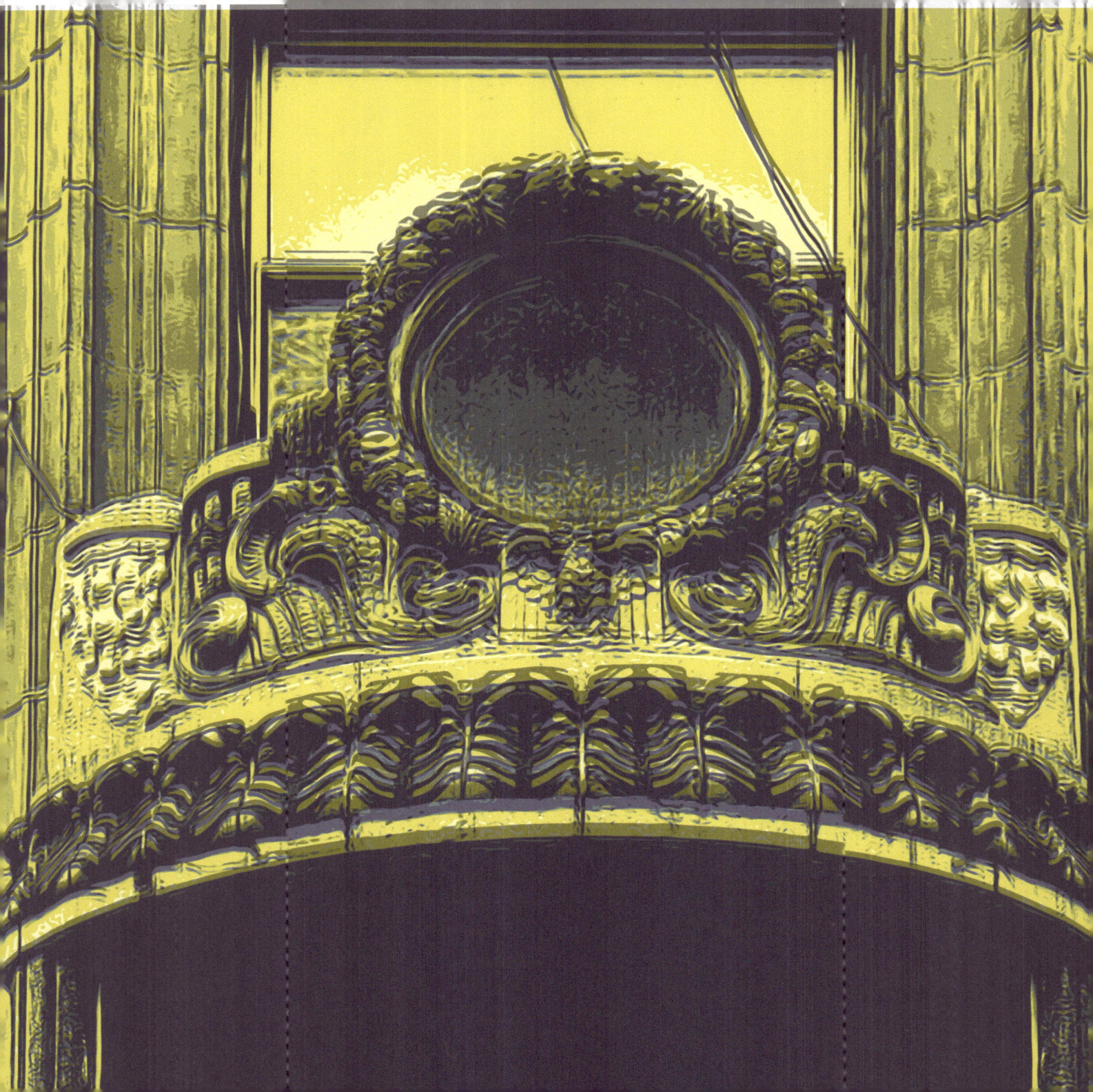

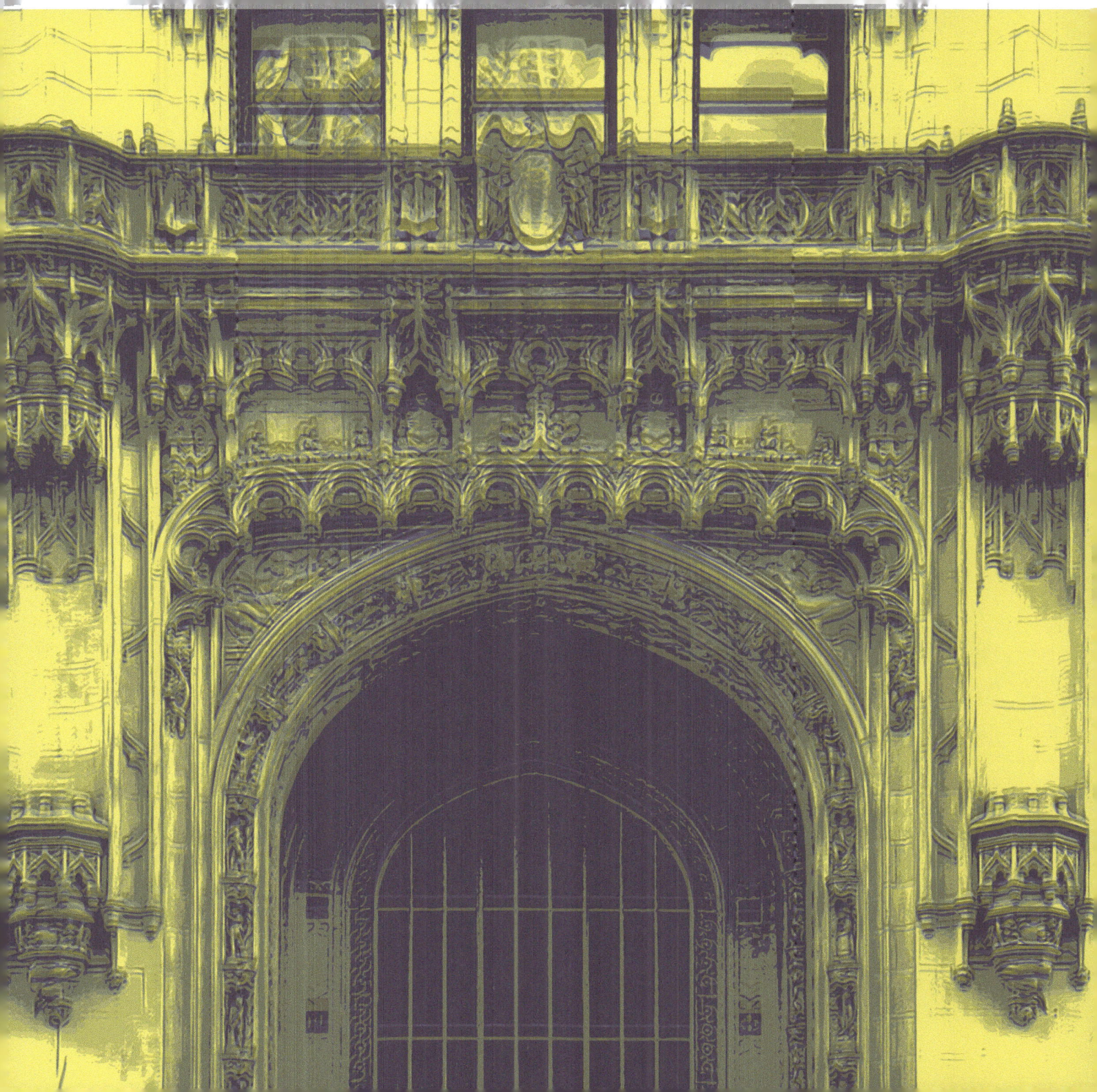

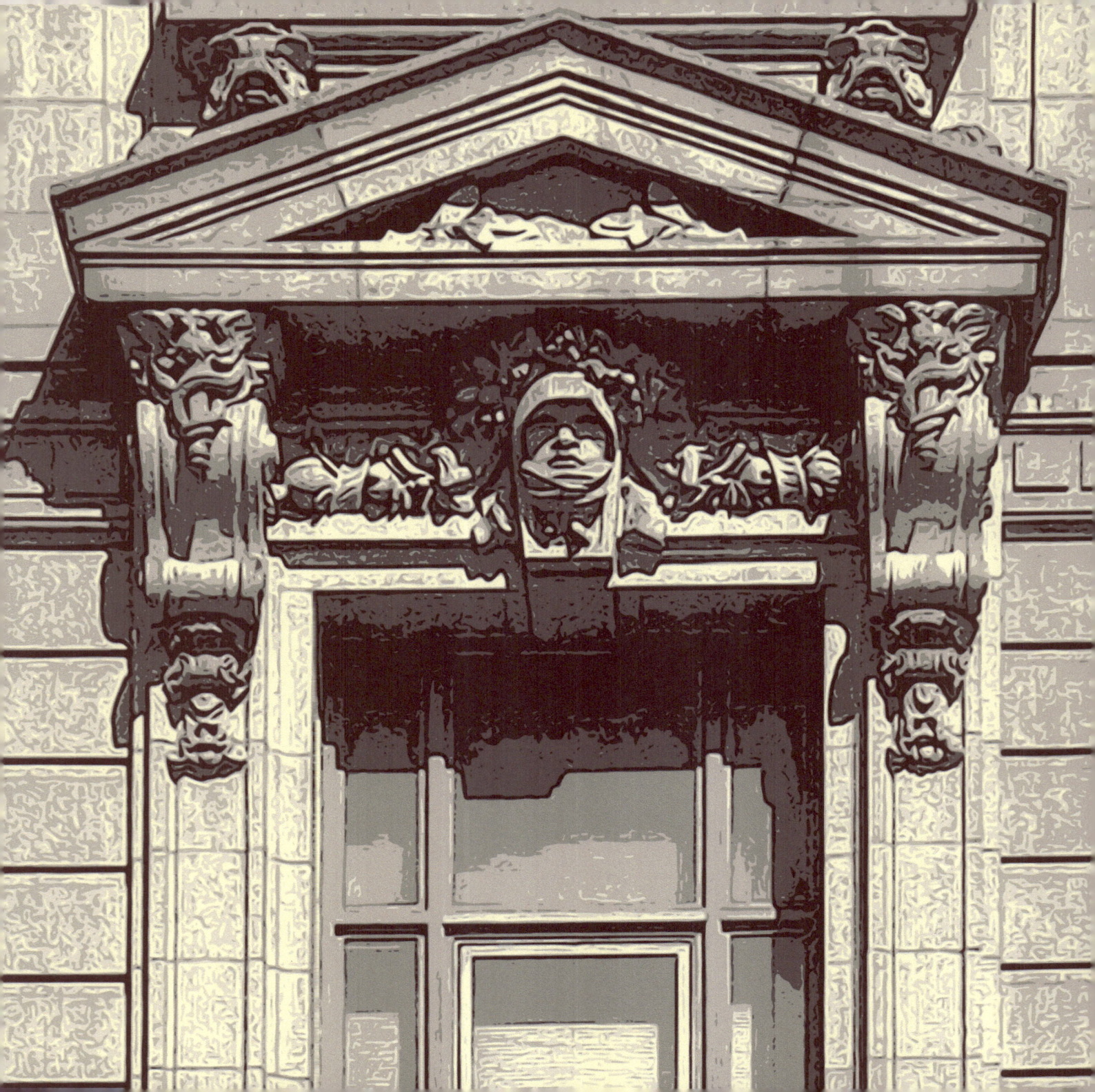

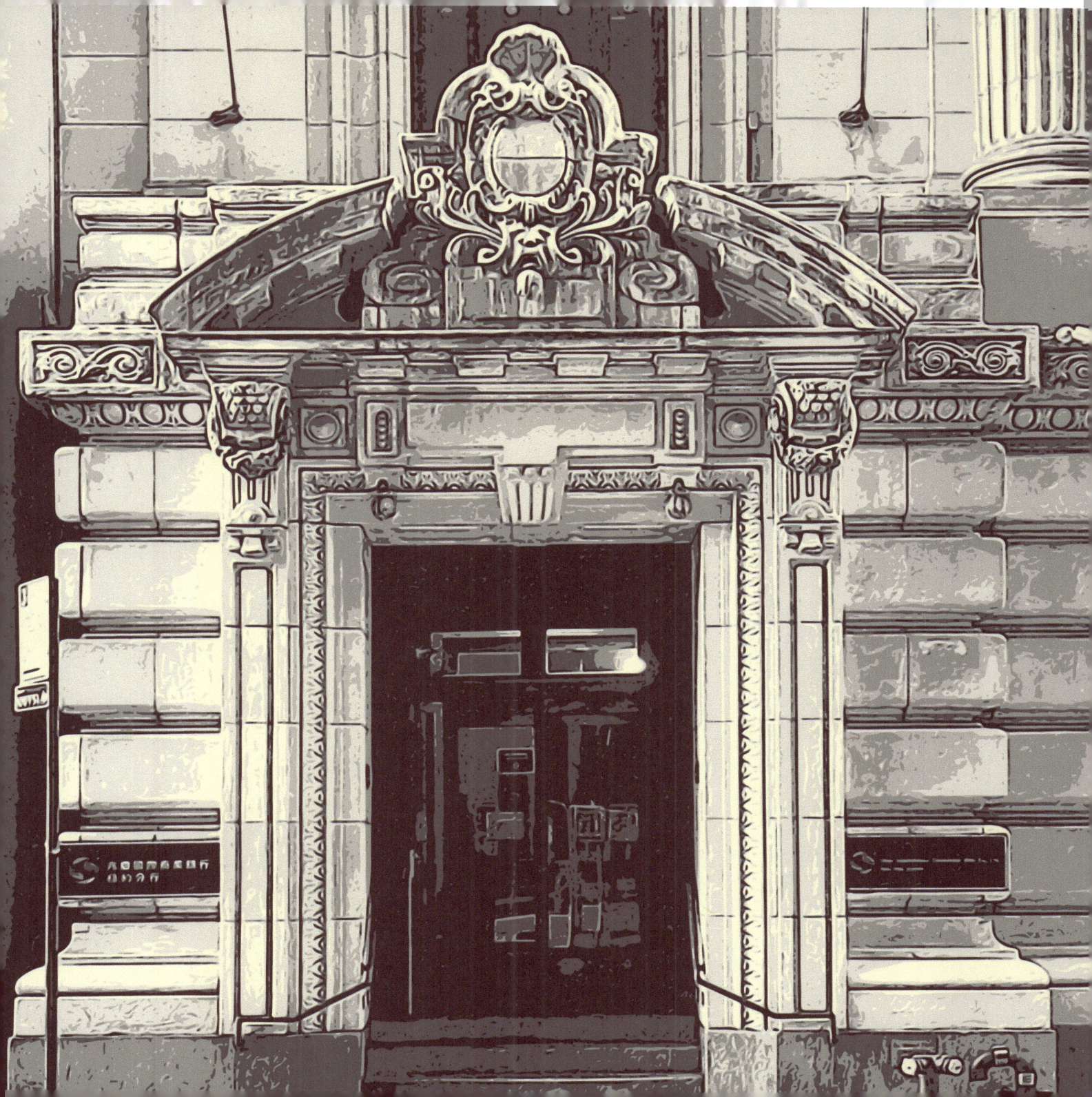

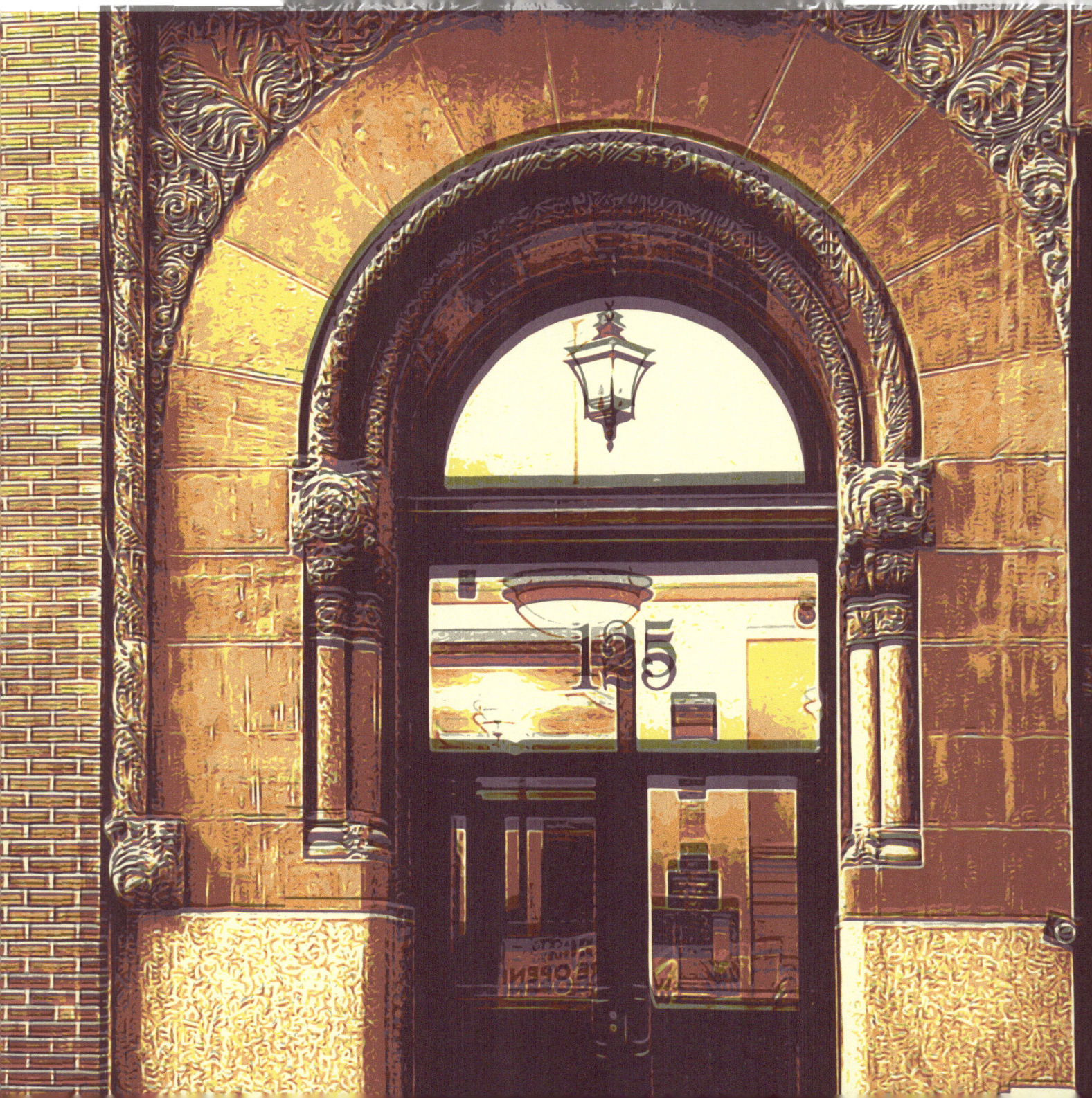

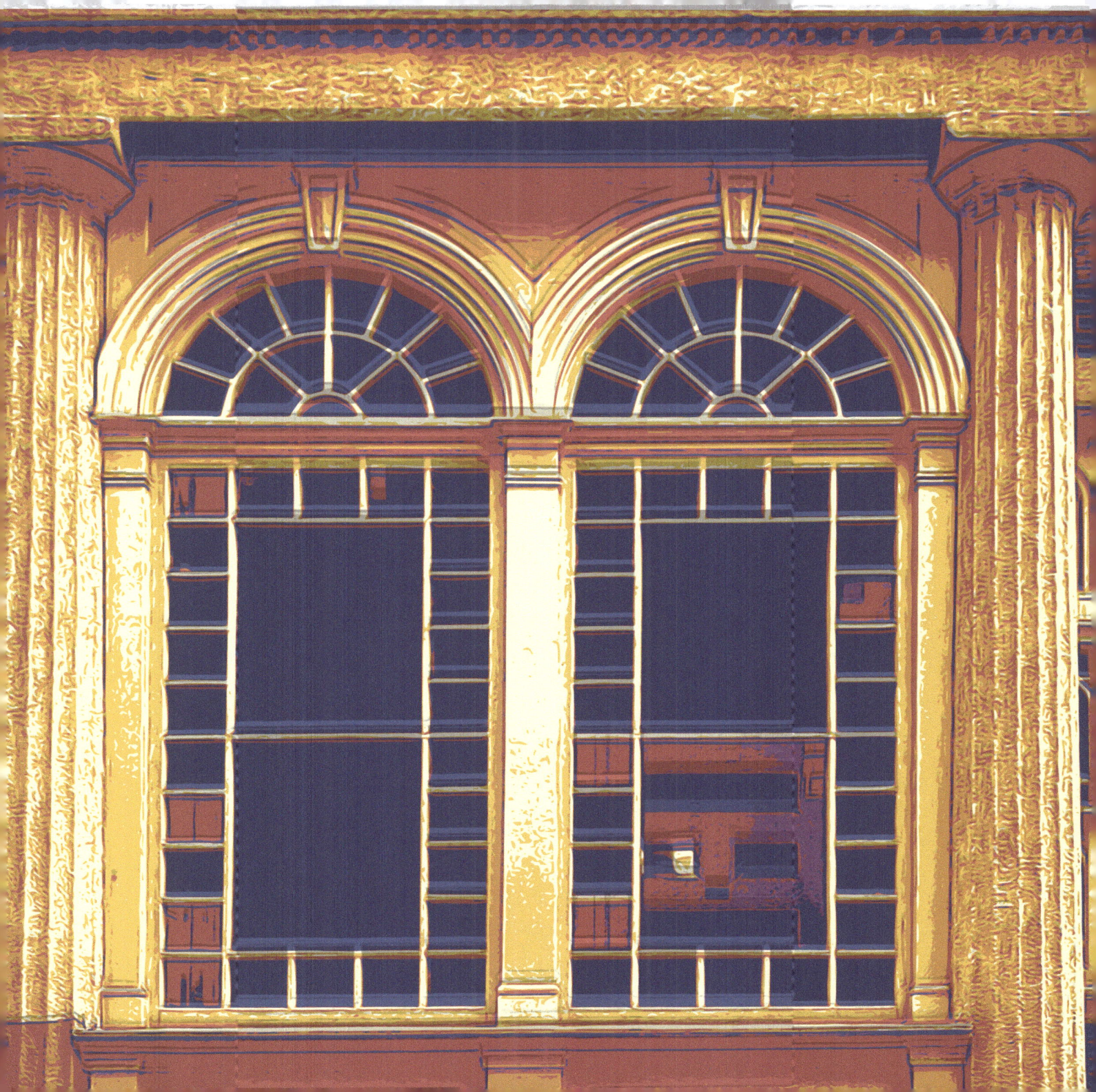

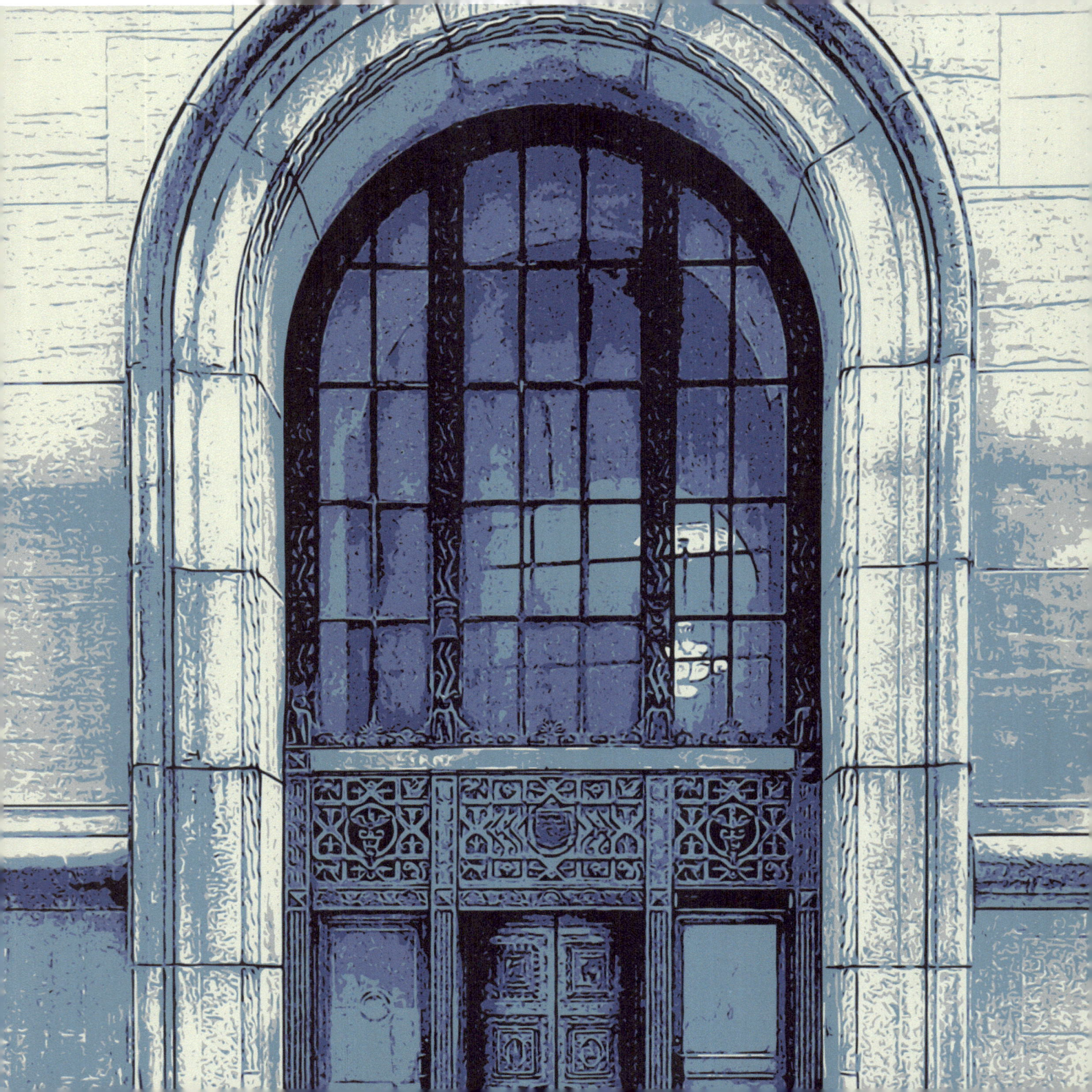

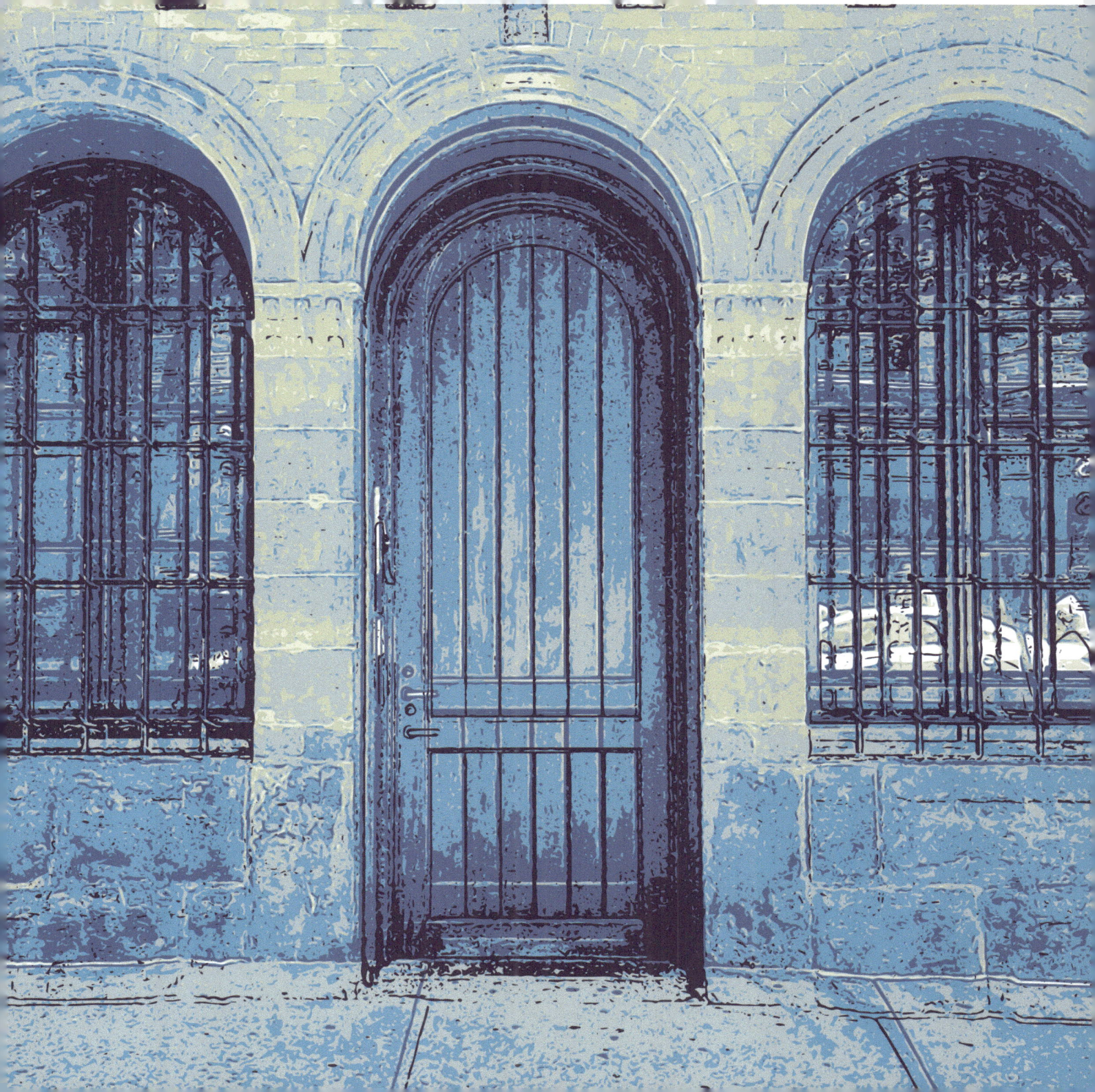

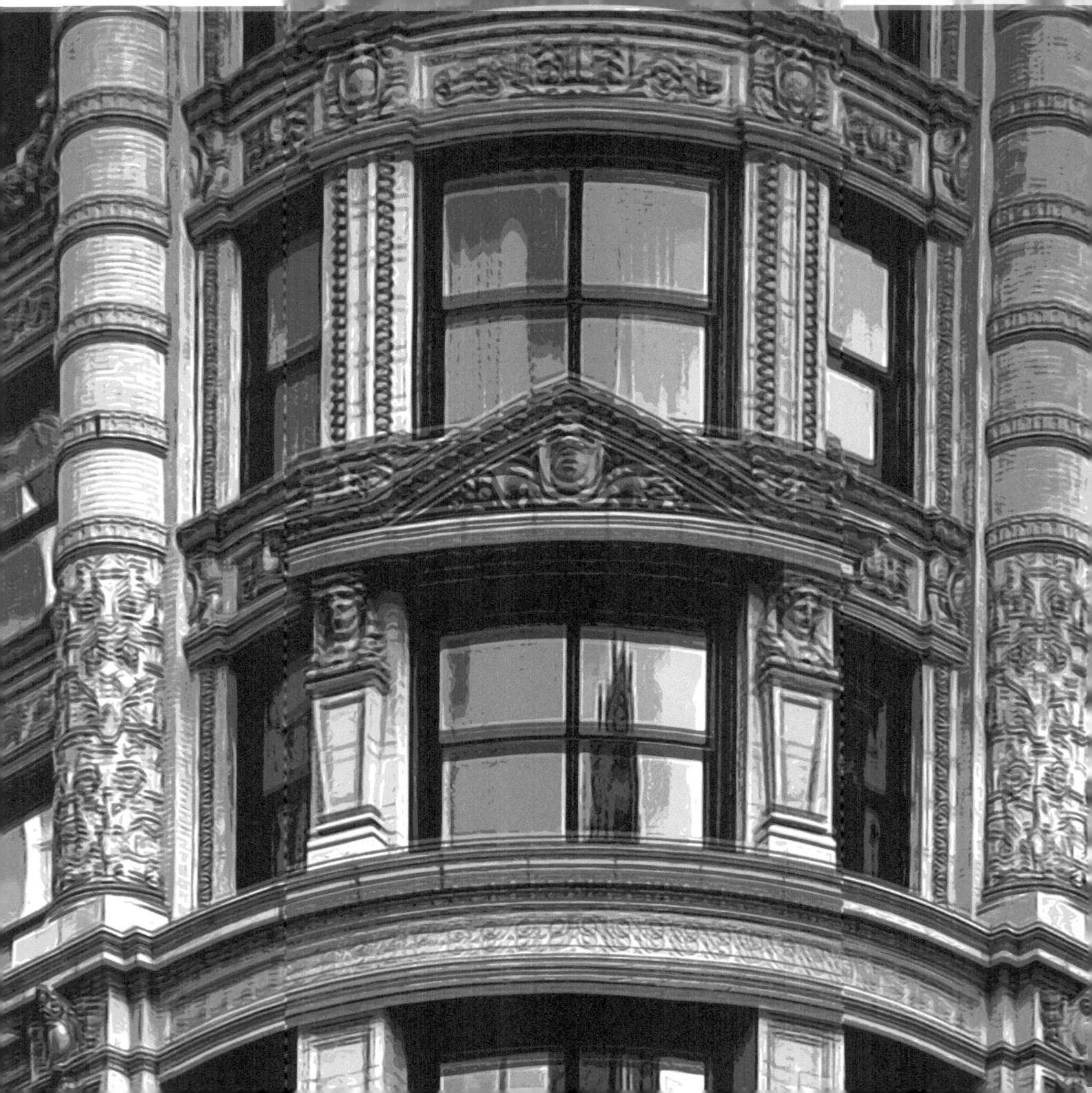

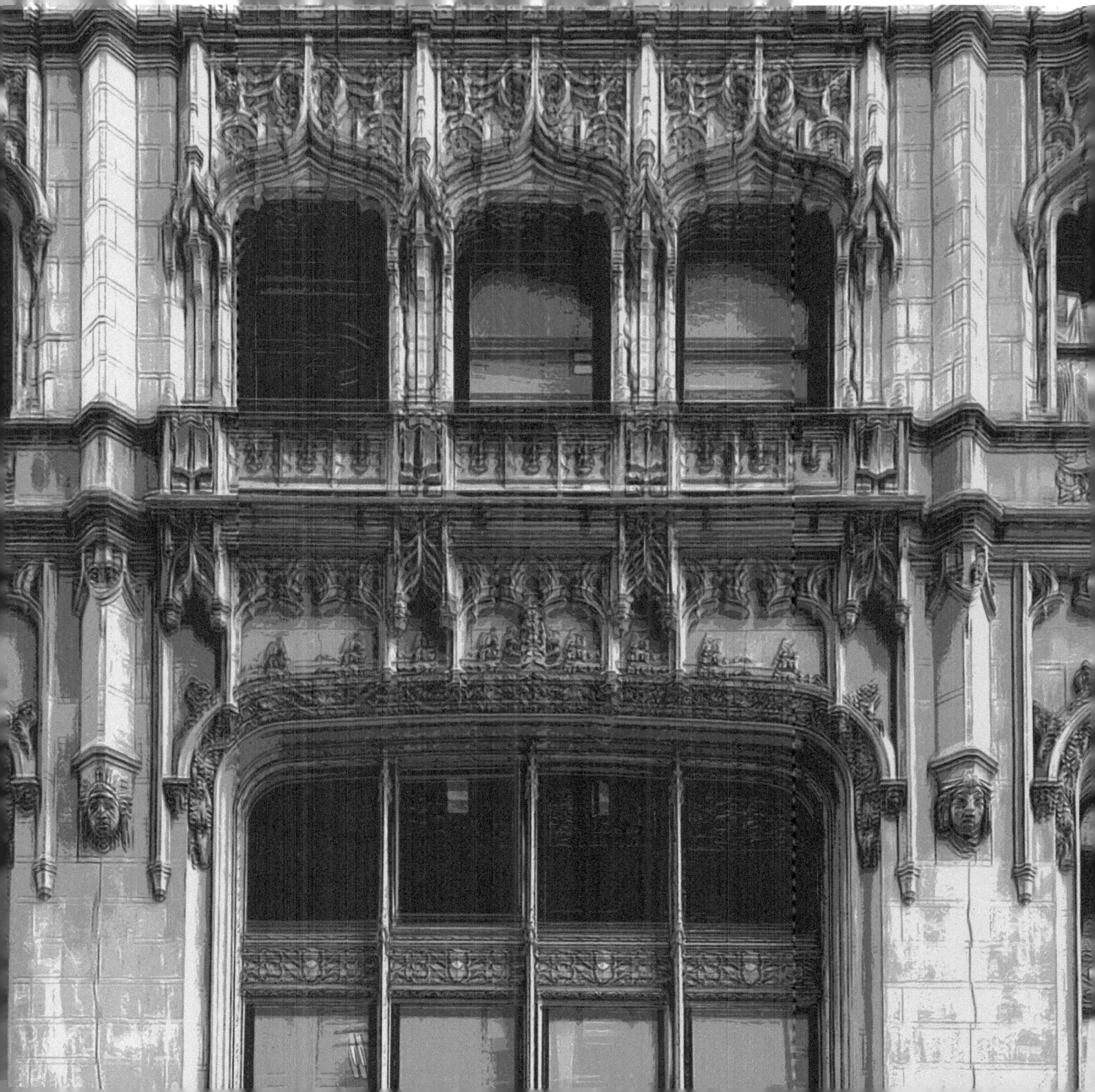

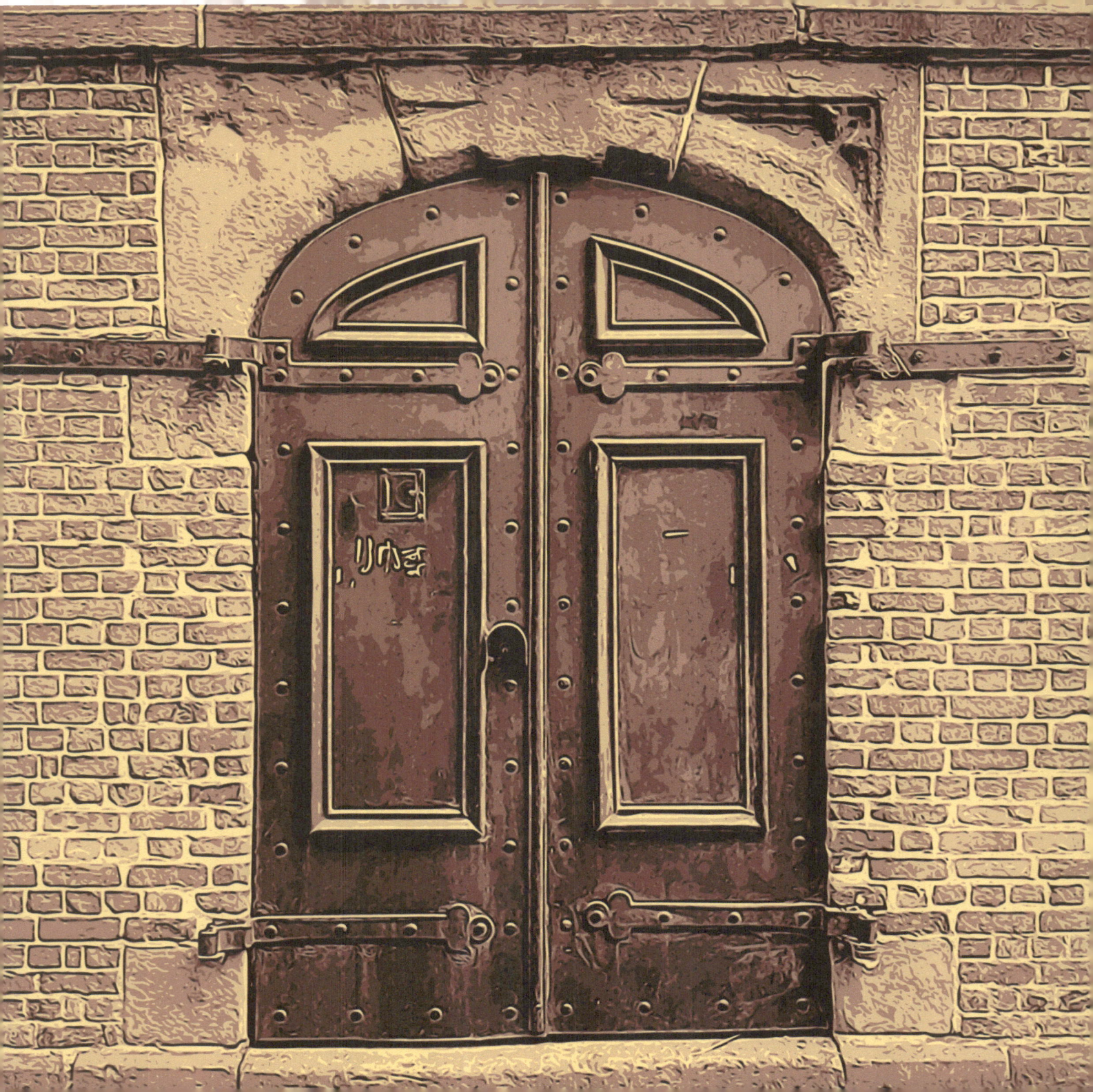

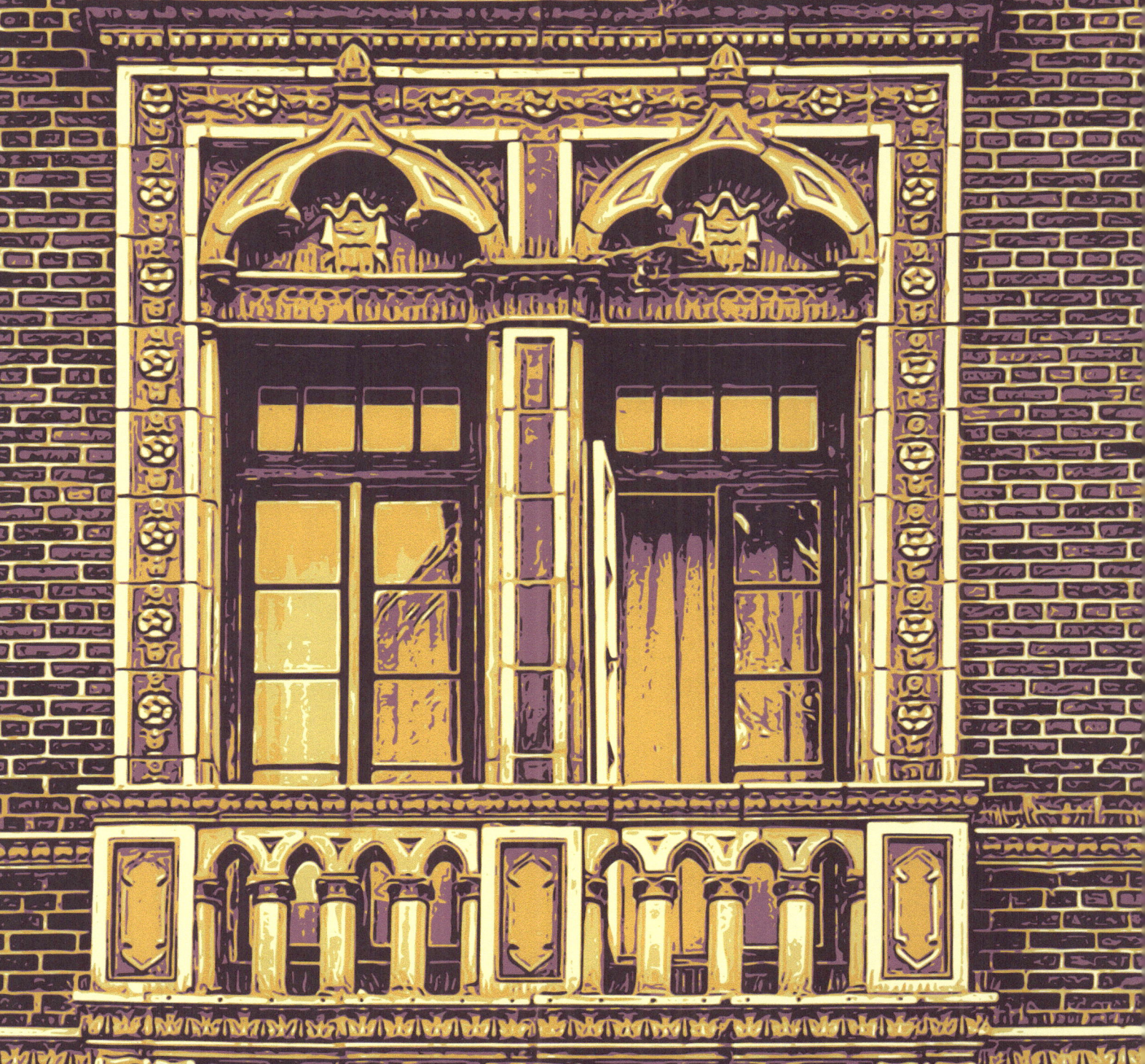

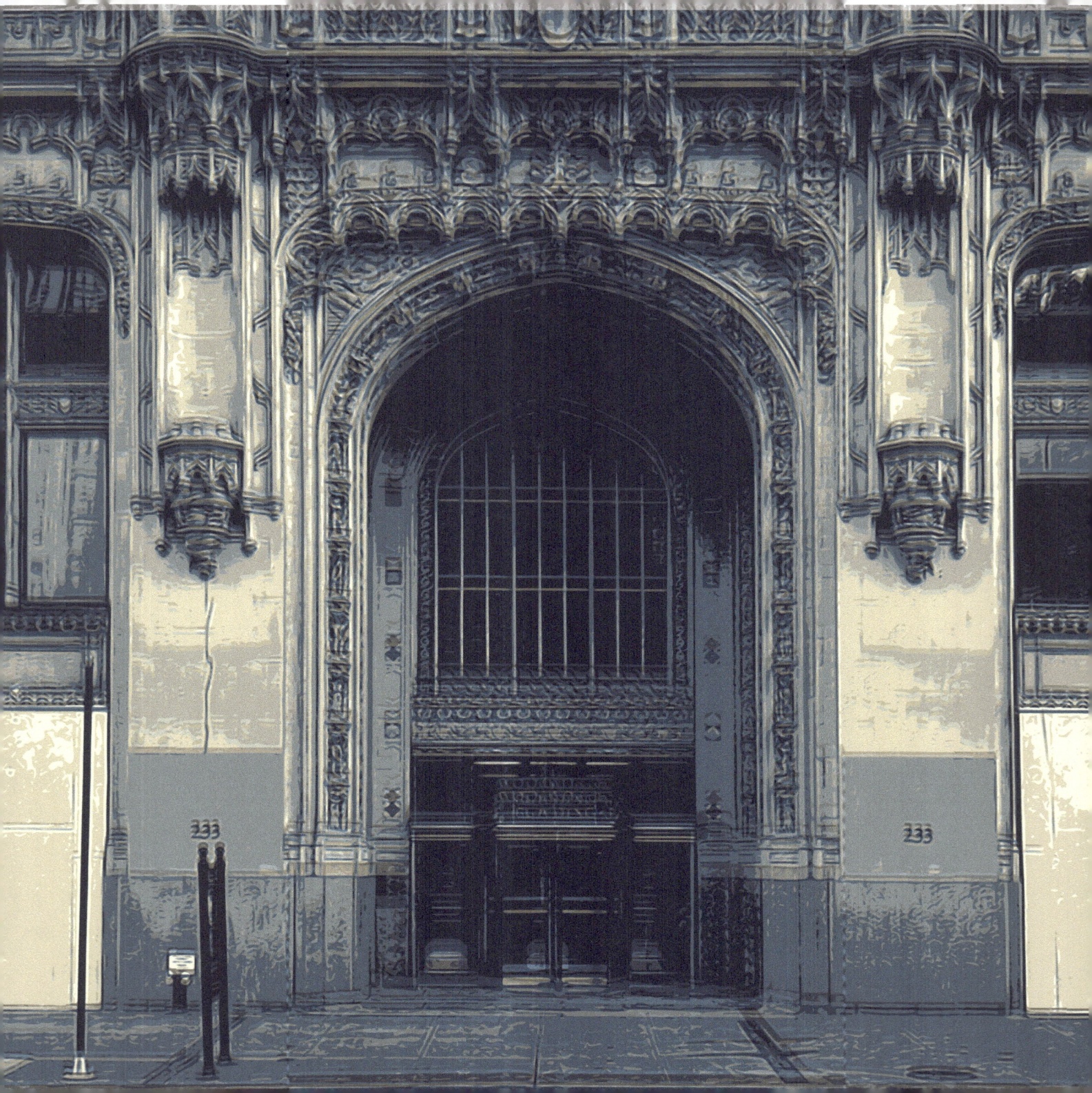

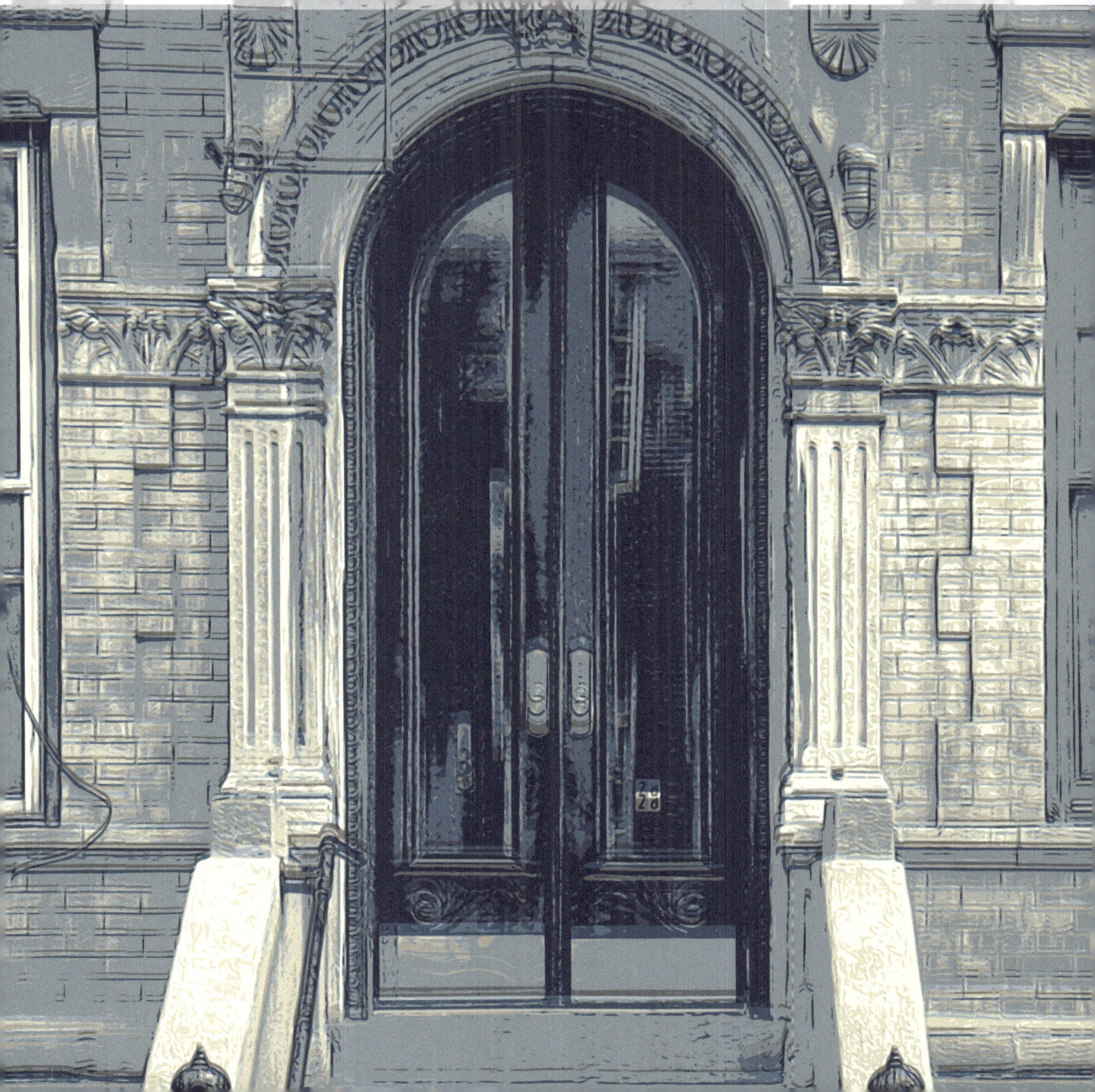

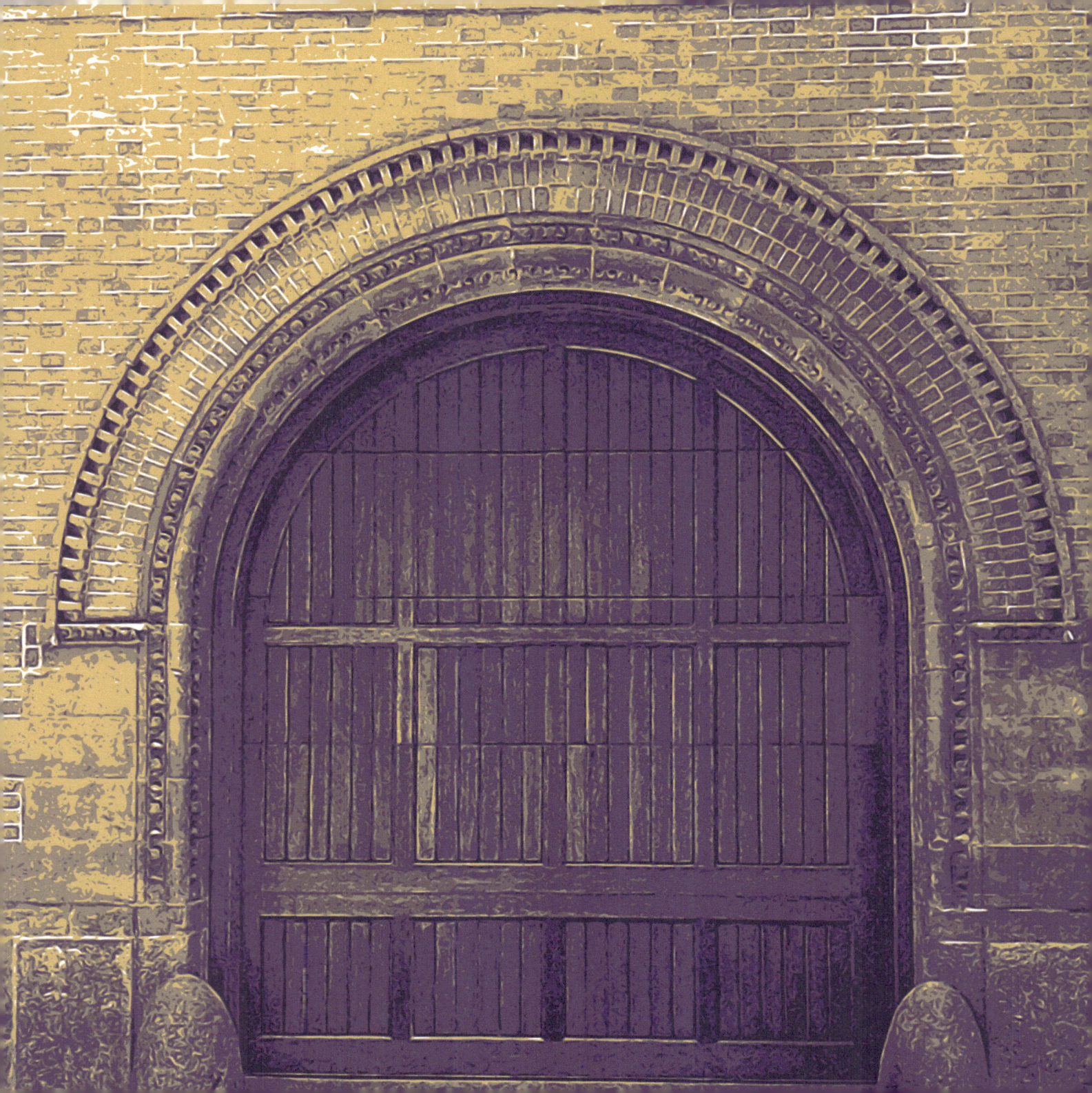

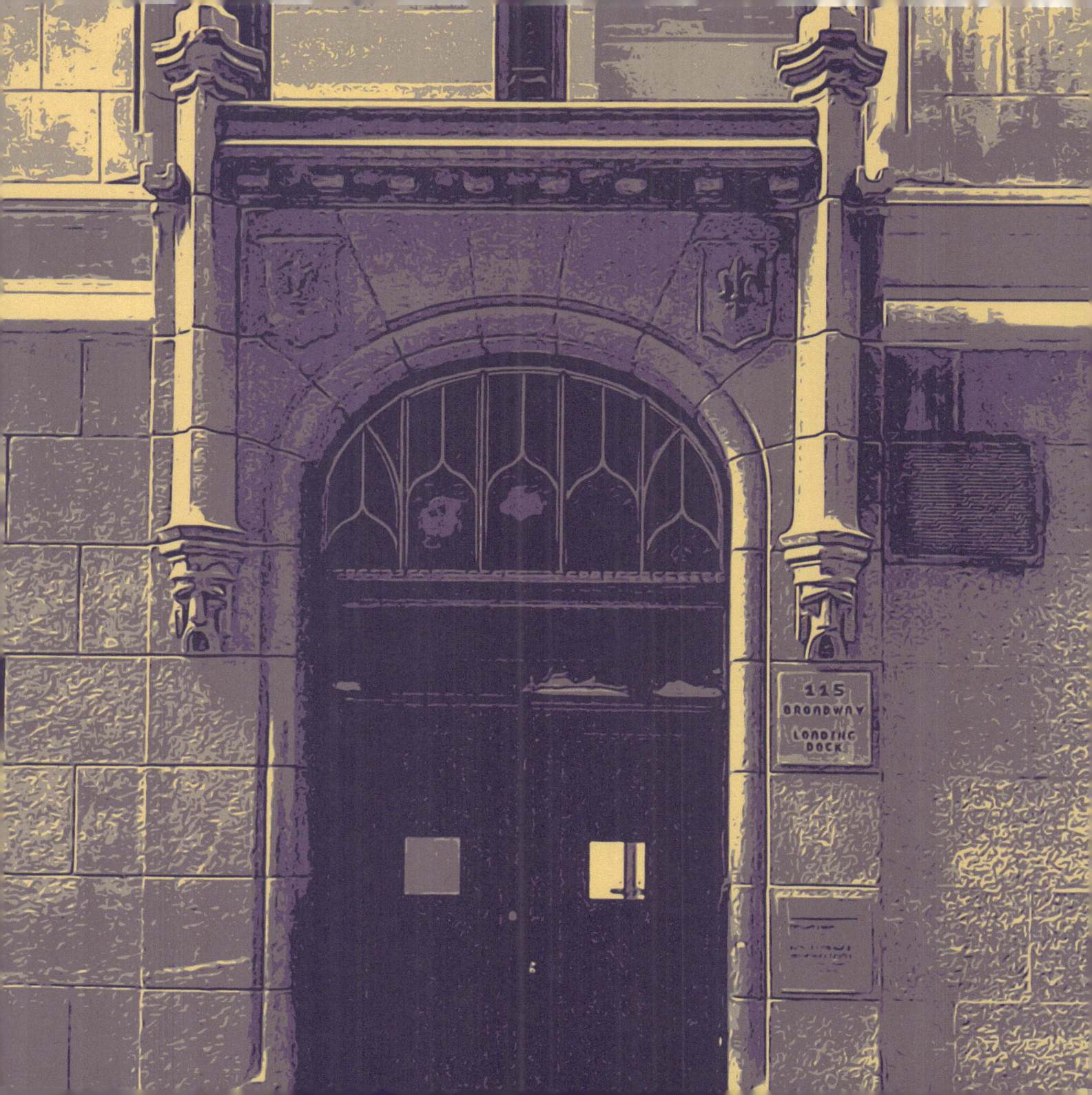

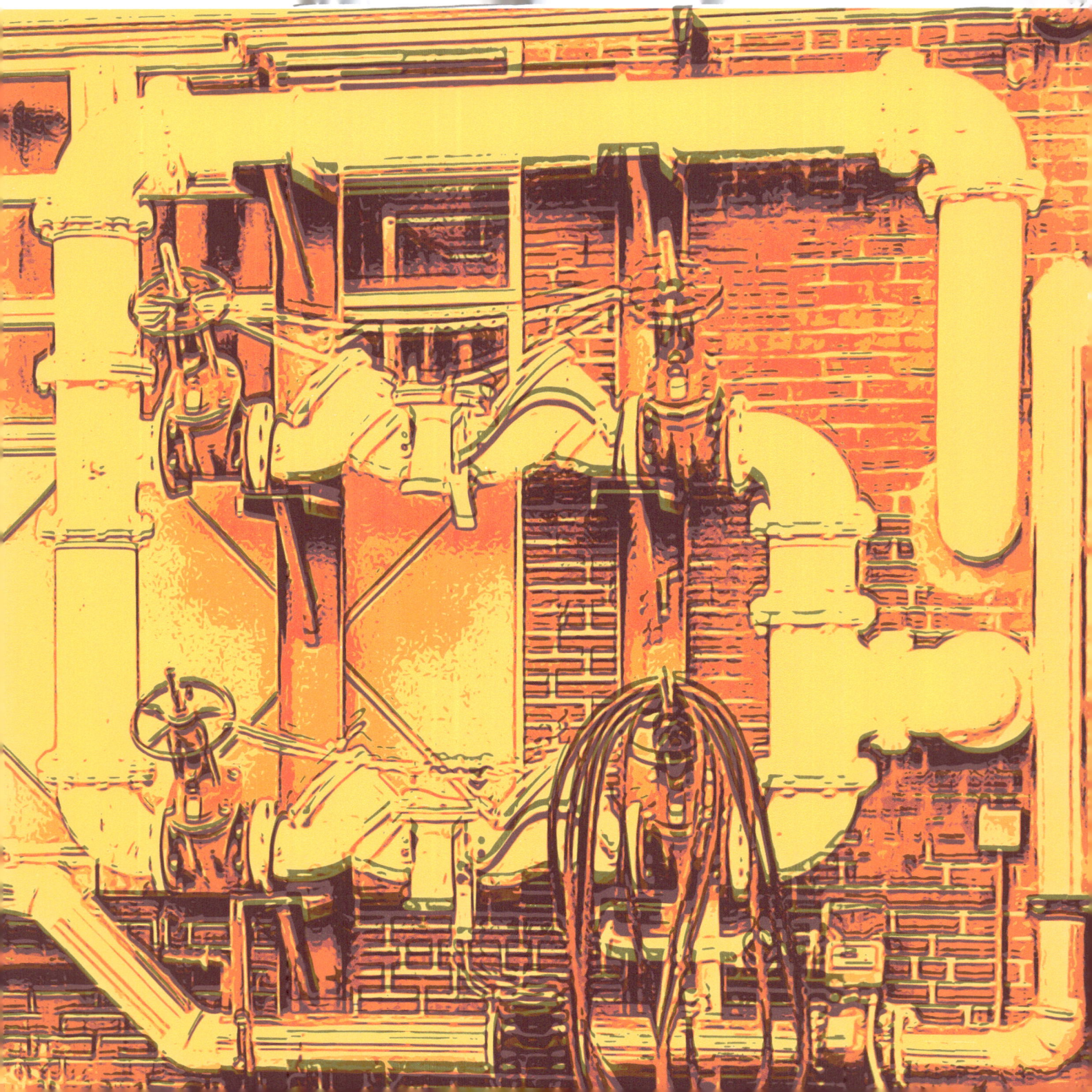

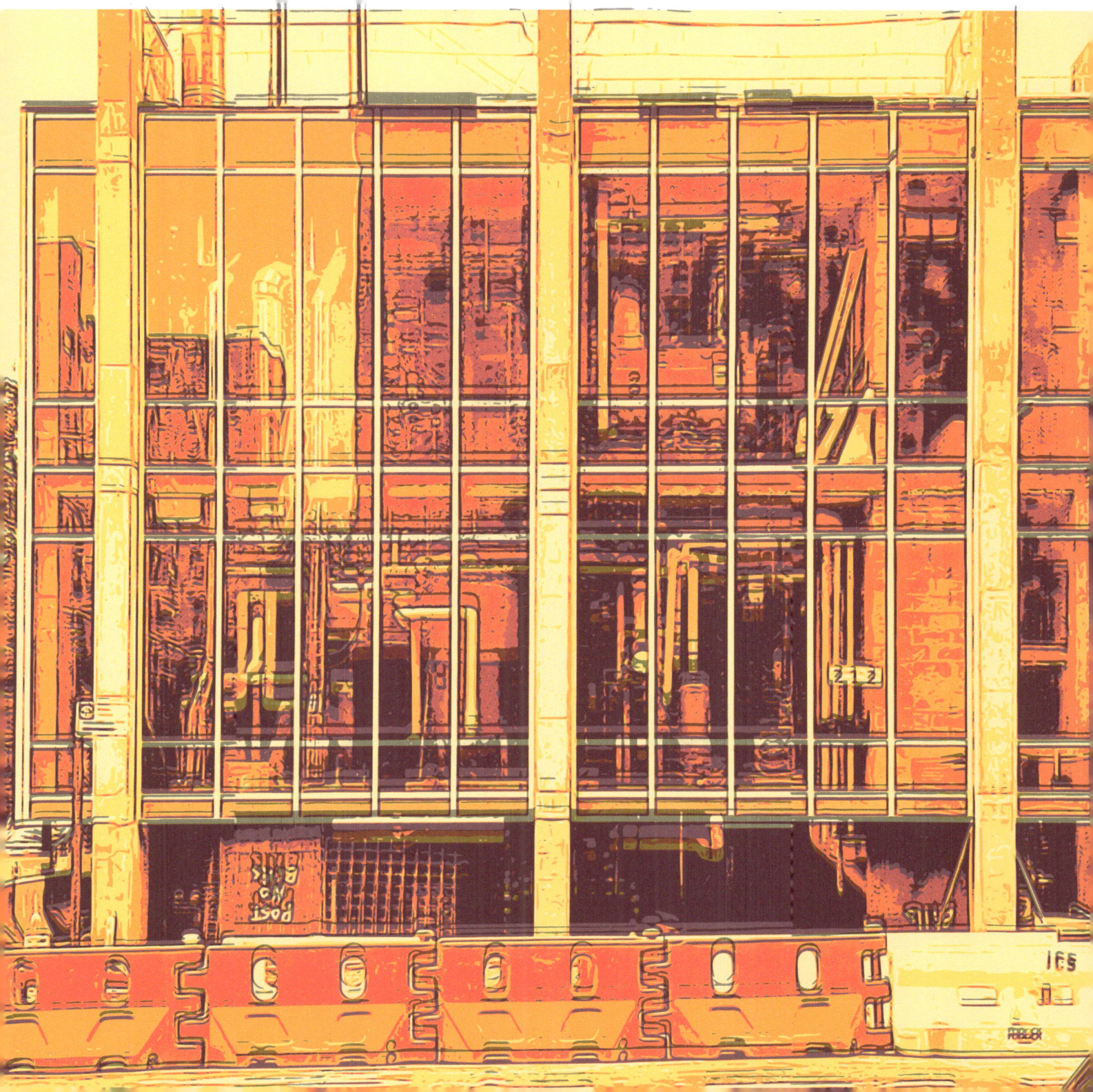

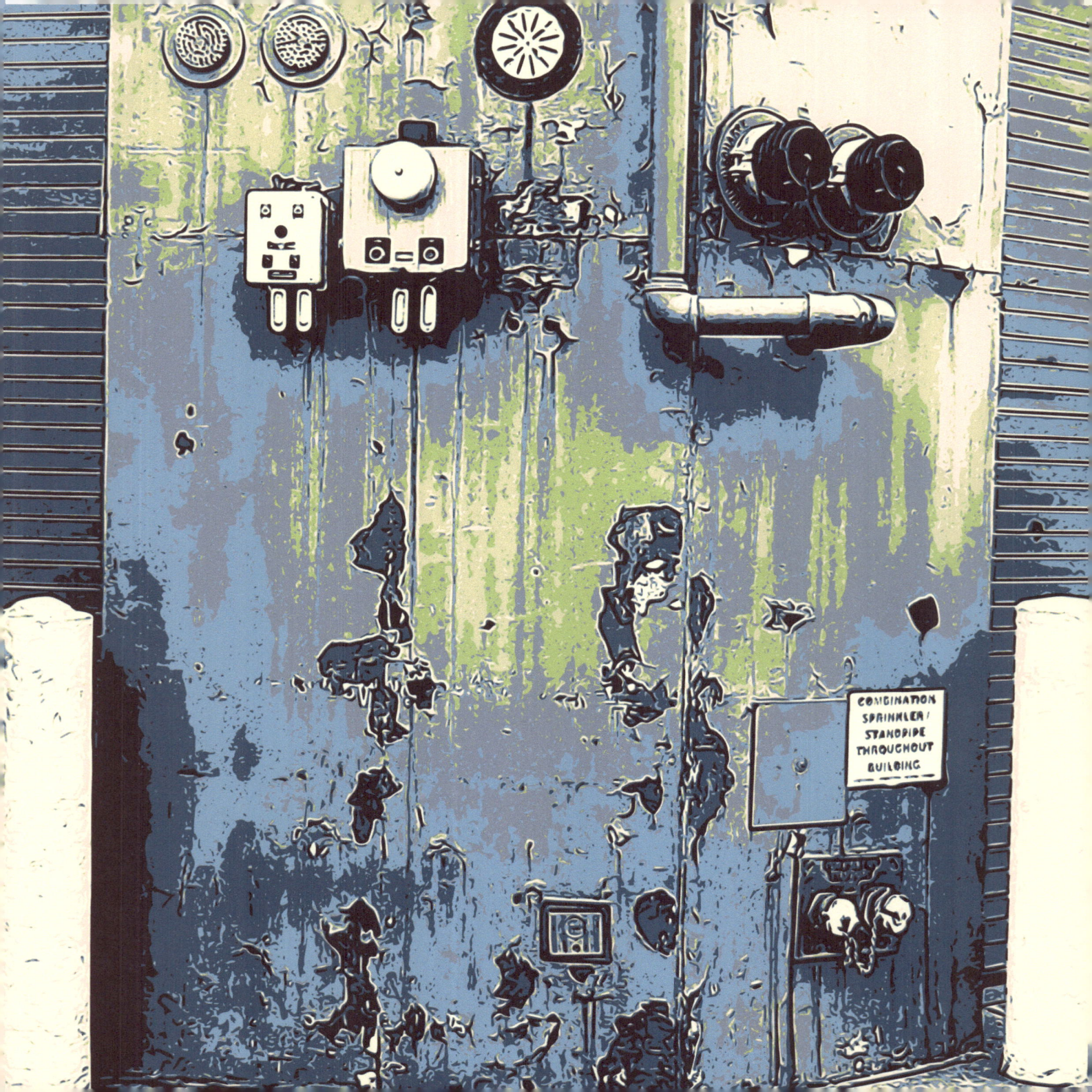

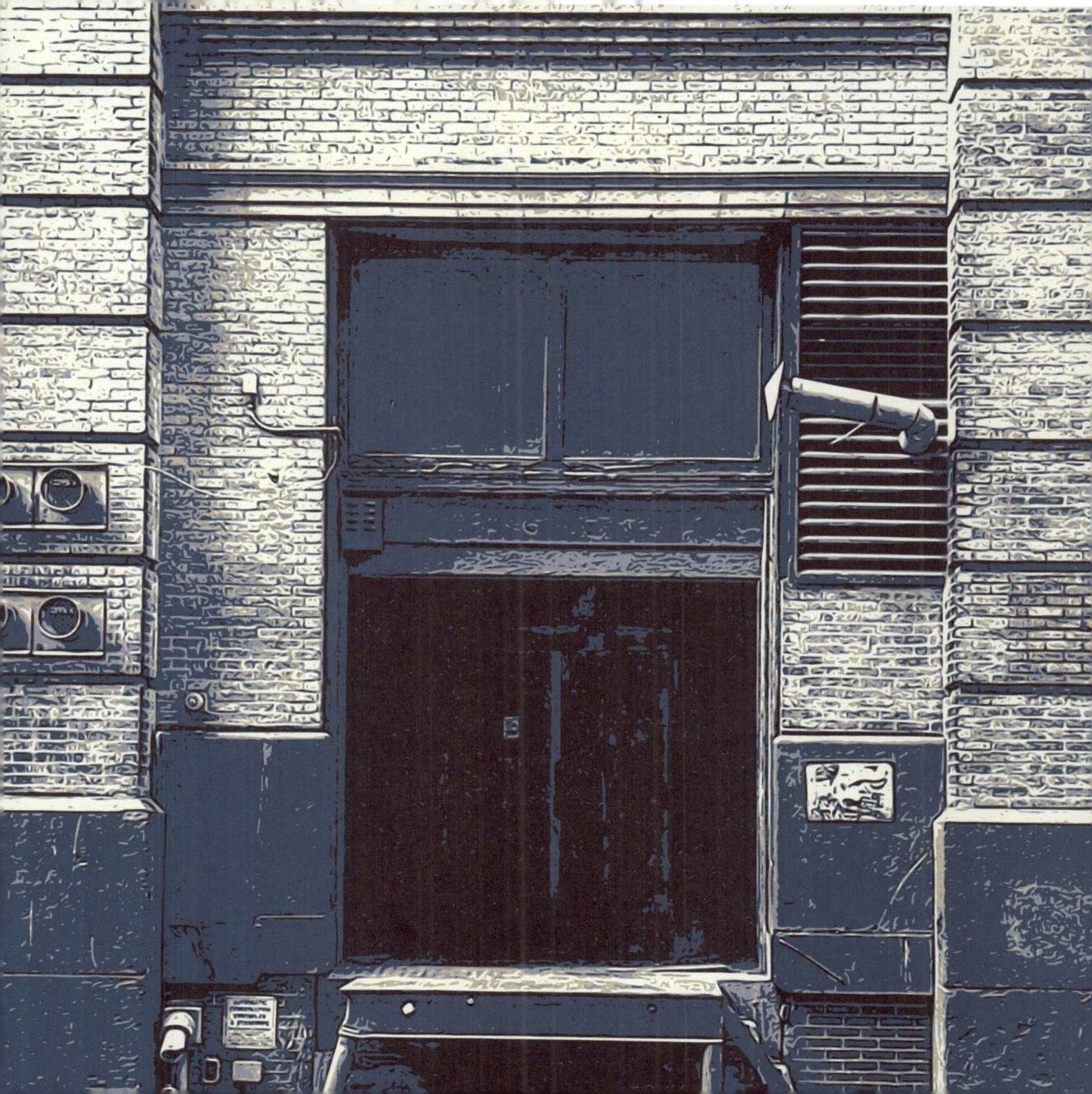

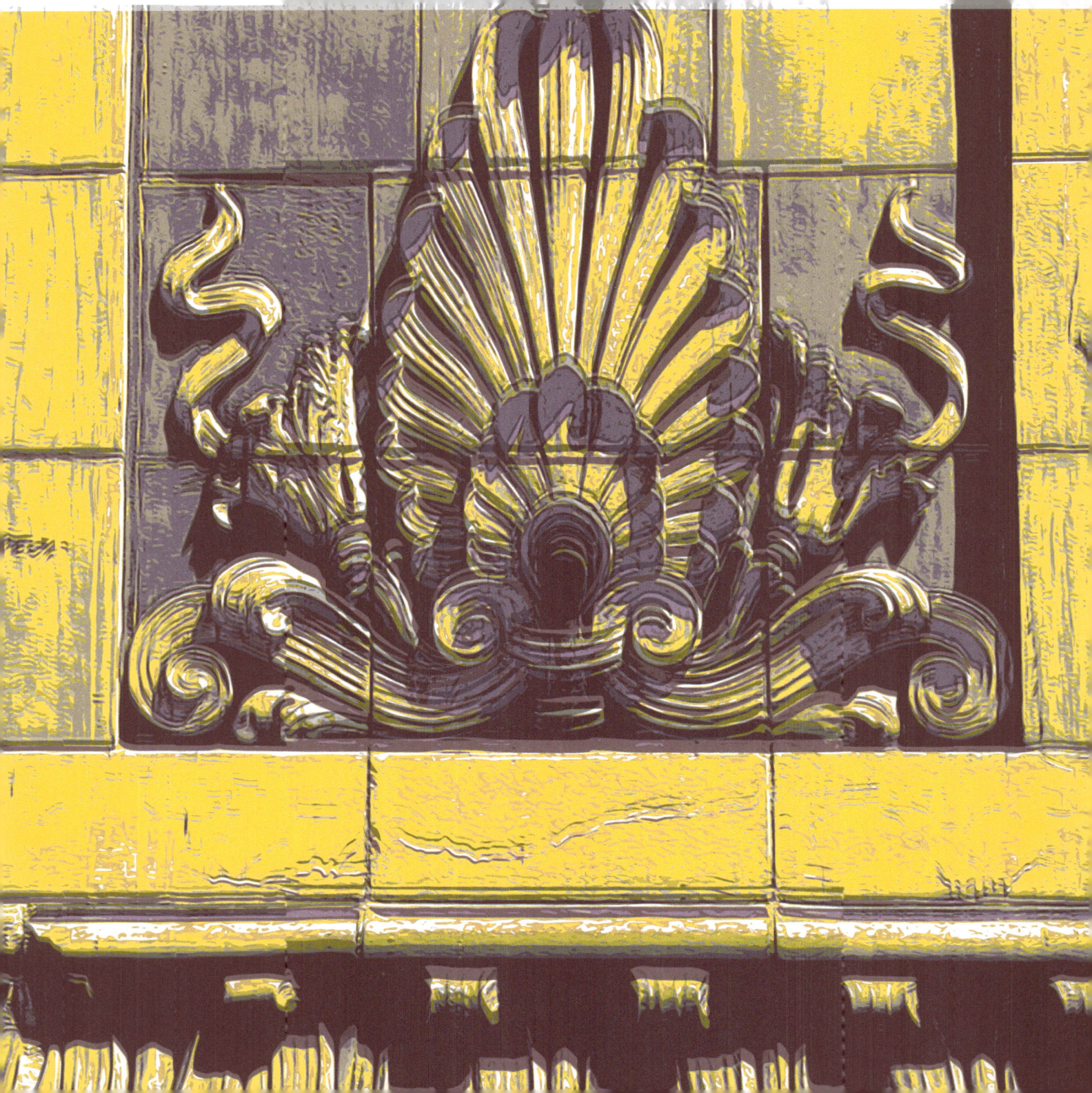

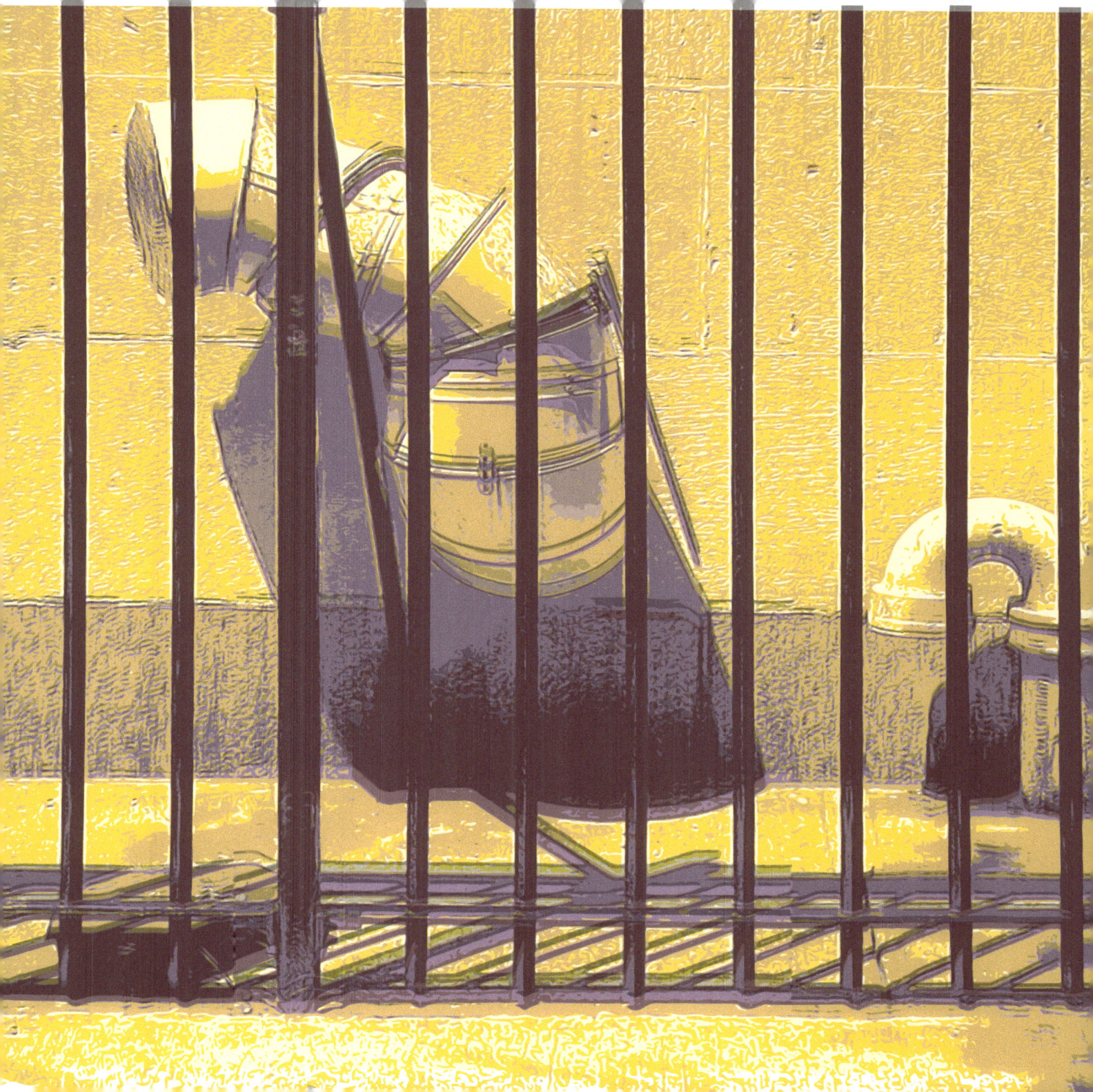

www.ingramcontent.com/pod-product-compliance
Lightning Source LLC
Chambersburg PA
CBHW051928210526
45473CB00006B/2180